COMPUTER MANAGEMENT

COMPUTER MANAGEMENT
A Common Sense Approach

NANCY FOY

FIRST EDITION

AUERBACH®
publishers

philadelphia
new york
london

Auerbach Publishers Inc.,
Philadelphia, 1972

in memory of
JOHN BOYER SURR
who would have approved

Contents

Preface

Computer users are no longer second-class citizens. During the 1970s more of them will realize that they actually control their own destinies. They also control the destiny of the computer industry.

Computer manufacturers have made huge technical advances in the past 25 years, but only now are the effects of their inbred attitudes coming to light. There may be a silent mass of contented computer users. If so, they aren't bothering to say so. The users we hear from are angry, frustrated, resigned, satirical, but always articulate. Their dissatisfaction is speeding up the demand for independent software, training, and many other forms of computer consulting.

Pendulum-like, the market obeys the laws of physics. When the mass of users grows and the level of friction rises, the users can bring about a deadly inertia—they stop buying so many computers. This has already begun in the United States and Britain, as the economic machinery itself slowed down and forced many to look at alternatives to new computers.

Unlike the pendulum, this trend away from computers may be self-sustaining. Computing won't stop, but the brute-force, indiscriminate application of computer power is already changing. The return to good times is not likely to bring a return to overbuying an overwhelming number of maxicomputers.

I believe the center of gravity in the computer industry is steadily and permanently shifting away from the mainframes and toward an expanding spectrum of services and do-it-yourself kits. IBM itself helped start this inexorable movement when it announced plans to unbundle the charges for software and service from the hardware.

Already there are indications of softer hardware—and harder software—as the manufacturers themselves try to keep up with the changing times. Eventually the user pressure may force all computer makers to provide machines with a common instruction set—a universal machine language. This could lift competition from the computer itself to the "firmware": plug-in instruction sets, or even entire applications.

The computer now accounts for perhaps one-third the cost of a system. Peripherals, software, training, consulting, and other services make up the other two-thirds. This ratio will move toward 25:75 by 1980.

Long after the computer is installed, even after it is paid for, the service costs continue. Technologists have done a great deal to bring down the cost per bit of computing, storage, and data communications. Businessmen should note that *managers* will have to take the initiative if the soaring personnel costs are to be kept under control. This book is simply a distillation of the common sense approaches that some successful data processing (DP) managers, line managers, and computer consultants have evolved to make it possible and sometimes pleasant to live with computers.

There's a serious reason for the automotive analogy that permeates the book. First, the computer industry, losing its glamour, is nonetheless growing and will become almost as large as the auto industry in a few years—and almost as mundane. Second, it makes sense to view the computer in the same perspective that we now view the car—useful, expensive, a convenience, an instrument for profound social change, a status symbol, a personal expression, a business necessity, the product of a maturing, important, and sometimes troubled industry.

In the words of Brian Brough (head of Management Services at BEA): "The computer bandwagon has been an impressive vehicle, with elegant styling and sumptuous interiors. But people are beginning to realize it has poor steering and no brakes."

Though the rise of computer sales may not keep pace with the manufacturers' predictions, the number of companies that use computers is rising astronomically. In the United States alone, 1.5 million corporate entities already use some form of computing, from tiny payrolls to cybernetic factories. The blurring of formerly sharp distinctions between accounting machines, in-house computers, and bureau terminals will also bring an increase in the number of companies that are first-time computer users.

These new users may be encountering computer jargon for the first time. It is only a few miles from Madison Avenue to IBM headquarters at Armonk. Somehow, the computer industry spent the past 25 years blending a profusion of academic and advertising buzzwords into a technononsense that often defies translation. Initiates used to take great pleasure in their ability to talk this jargon and thus encouraged the secret language.

Now that the computer club is getting bigger, it is time to publish the secret words and the lessons learned in the painful initiation rites of the pioneers.

N.F.

Acknowledgments

It has been said (by Dr. Maurice Kendall) that the person who takes credit for a concept or theorem is usually the first one who neglected to attribute it to his predecessor. Let me make it clear at the outset that I am a journalist, not a technologist. I have tried to leave as many words of wisdom as possible in the mouths of the original wise men. Others have simply been assimilated too well.

More than concepts and theorems, I respect common sense. We have surprising quantities of it in the computer industry. In addition to Dr. Kendall, I am particularly grateful to Philip Dorn and Isaac Auerbach in the United States, who helped keep me in touch with American views; to Cameron Low for his advice on training; and to Ed Williams who suggested the book in the first place and then was generous with unbillable hours to review the manuscript and argue about everything therein, from management information to COM.

The editors of *New Scientist, Management Today,* and *Data Systems* in Britain have all been generous in giving permission to include material that was originally written for their journals.

Most of all, I am indebted to my IBM typewriter, which has demonstrated exceptional reliability and maintainability, and to my children Ann and John, who patiently put up with months of computer shoptalk, ran the household, administered scrambled eggs or coq au vin as necessary during the writing phase, and ceremoniously served me Soberano whenever a chapter finished itself.

London, 1972   Nancy Foy

1

Keeping the Manager in the Driver's Seat

When you buy a car, you have your own reasons for selecting a certain set of characteristics. It must be a station wagon, to carry the children and their gear, or a sporty model because you drive alone and enjoy cruising at high speed on the freeways. You decide to take the smaller motor to save money on fuel, or the bigger one because it gives you more power for passing. You choose a nice light beige because the dust won't show, or British racing green because it looks sporty. You have a selection of foreign and domestic models from the mini to the Mercedes.

When you get behind the wheel and turn the key, you expect the car to start. You drive purposefully from one place to another, expecting the car to turn the corner when you turn the steering wheel. You, not the car, choose the route.

The car can be a dangerous machine, so certain standards must be met before you take one out on the open road. The car must be mechanically sound, and you must prove your driving proficiency and knowledge of the laws. Nonetheless, you don't have to be an automotive engineer to drive it. You simply take driving lessons, or learn from another capable driver. If something goes wrong, you find a mechanic; and if he's good, you keep on going to him to keep the car running smoothly.

Why can't computers be like this?

They can, and should. But this won't happen until there is a critical mass of capable "drivers" who are making their needs known to the computer manufacturers and service people who design the machines and make them work.

In the earliest days of the automobile industry, the driver had to be his own mechanic. The general public was often alarmed by the noisy creatures that careened too fast down country lanes, scaring horses and kicking up dust. Then Henry Ford came along with his Model T. You could have any color you wanted, so long as it was black. But the cost was reasonable. Many families began to consider driving to the shore on a Sunday afternoon. More roads were built. More car companies began to furnish competitive wares, and an industry grew. Eventually it got out of hand, with too many manufacturers losing money, so the number of car makers dwindled, but not car usage. (To this day, they still make extravagant and misleading claims for their products. So do computer makers.) Finally, the buyer could have any color he wanted. The choice of cars began to include exotic sports cars and specially outfitted campers. Every town had a few garages and service stations. Cars began to be standardized—three or four gears instead of six, for example—as more people learned how to drive.

MODEL T COMPUTER USERS

We've just about reached the Model T stage in the evolution of computer use. From now on it will be up to the users to learn to drive competently, to push for standardization, and to demand what they want from the computer industry, refusing to buy until they get it.

The computer industry is not just IBM, any more than the automobile industry is just General Motors. It consists of thousands of companies. Only 20 or so are major computer manufacturers, and their number is already dwindling. Several hundred more make small computers or specialized systems. Hundreds more make the terminals and peripheral equipment that put information into the computers and take it out again. In the United States alone there are over 1000 service bureaus, 2500 software companies, 7500 consulting firms, 200 leasing companies, and hundreds of accessory manufacturers, training schools, and used-computer companies, not to mention the hundreds of universities and research institutions that are exploring the computer and its uses. The U.S. computer industry had gross revenues of at least $12 billion in 1970. Estimates of a ten-fold increase by 1980 are not unusual. The business of manipulating and communicating information is likely to be the world's largest industry within a few years.

Why is it, then, that the simplest computerized accounting system costs ten times the original estimate and still doesn't work properly after several years?

Why are companies spending a fortune to get better management information, but failing to use it effectively in decision making?

Why are administration costs rising instead of falling?

Why are most installations a dead loss when it comes to making a return on investment? The A. J. Kearney consulting firm reported in 1970 that the average computer performs productive work only 48 percent of the time.

A survey of the computer industry in Britain's *Economist* in February 1971 said that business organizations are losing hundreds of millions of dollars on their computers every year. "Many senior executives now regard their computer systems as the worst investments their companies have ever made," it commented.

The new president of Aerojet-General Corporation in California in 1971 threw out the computers that linked his nine major divisions, on the premise that people do a better job of running companies than computers do. He felt that computers sap the motivation and intelligence of people who should be making decisions, and instead turn them into information processors.

The reasons for most computer debacles lie not in technical matters but human ones. Broadly, they boil down to optimism, ostrichism, and isolation.

TECHNICAL RENAISSANCE

The first electronic computer, Mark I, was developed by IBM and Harvard University just as World War II was coming to an end. The war gave a tremendous impetus to technology on all fronts—machines for production, jet aircraft, new plastics, atomic power, rockets, synthetic fibers, electronics.

It is not surprising that the first computer people had to develop a new vocabulary to describe their machines and what they could do. They worked in milliseconds and later microseconds, solving precise scientific formulas that translated fairly simply into the positive and negative electrical impulses that the computer could handle. The computer men and their machines even worked in an entirely different number system called *binary*. Because the computer recognized only circuits that were "on" or "off," the computer people adjusted their own ways of counting. Thus, instead of:

0	they counted	0
1		1
2		10
3		11
4		100
5		101
6		110
7		111
8		1000
9		1001
10		1010

Most schoolchildren learn the binary number system (or any other) fairly easily. Adults who have always lived in an orderly business world in which it was possible to count on one's fingers, a world in which the multiplication tables were an absolute verity, find binary much more difficult.

Several of the early computer men saw immediately that their machines would have broad use in business because they could calculate so rapidly and handle such huge quantities of information. Airlines were among the earliest commercial users. Imaginative businessmen also saw the potential, and a few installed systems to handle particular jobs. These machines, specially designed for their tasks, were originally "hard-wired" to shunt the zeros and ones around on specific paths to do certain calculations in a certain order, working from information fed in with a very rigid format.

The optimism that led to many of today's computer problems is characteristic of any young industry, created and expanded by young men. In this case they were young men with highly technical training and, as a result, very little chance for experience in traditional business organizations. The advances they made in technology were spectacular. From a collection of slow, hot, and cumbersome vacuum tubes, computers evolved into smaller, transistorized machines that could do much more work, in less time, in a smaller space, for a lower cost. Finally, microcircuits made it possible to put a middle-sized computer into a drawer in a secretary's desk.

Even the technologists underestimated the speed of their own technical advances. People also underestimated the impact these machines would have on human life and on business life. Similarly, nobody in the 1920s could have envisaged the 1970 city, choking in its own smog, constricted by its freeway system, with congestion on its broad avenues sometimes bringing all traffic to a complete standstill.

In 1952 author Kurt Vonnegut, Jr. published an Orwellian book called *Player Piano,* in which he foresaw a society with completely automated factories producing all goods and a benign central computer taking all government decisions while a telegenic figurehead of a president made folksy speeches to keep down trouble in the bored population. Vonnegut's automated factories have not yet come to pass and are unlikely to do so. But his policy-making computer, depicted as a mass of tubes and wires filling the vast Carlsbad Caverns of New Mexico, could probably be housed now in the average company's computer room. It is unlikely now that computers will ever determine national policies, although Russia is working on a massive project to do its long-range planning based on a computerized model of the entire population.

THE COMPUTER ORGANIZATION

Another thing the technologists consistently underestimated (and still seem to underestimate) is the human and organizational difficulties that stand between the sale of a computer and its ability to do the job for which it was purchased.

Most people in company management reacted to the computer and its complexities with ostrich-like attitudes. Certainly computers were the coming thing. But if they tried asking why a new system that cost half a million was imperative, the answers they got from their technologists were so flowery with technical words and so incomprehensible in business terms that most top managers stopped asking, and simply avoided the job of evaluating the matter—characteristically pushing it down the line to a computer man.

Most of these computer men, especially in the early years, were better equipped with pioneering spirit and professional elitism than business judgment and experience or company loyalty. Larger and larger systems were thus created to do professionally challenging jobs rather than cost-effective ones. The blame must be shared. Computer departments were often left to work in isolation, outside the mainstream of corporate life.

The bigger their systems got, the more likely they were to involve an army of suppliers, consultants, and software houses to create the individual instructions that were beginning to be necessary for each system to do its different tasks. As the computer makers tried to generalize their scientific machines into being all things to all users, computer languages began to proliferate. These, too, were overgeneral and underuseful. Administration —another matter in which computer experts were normally untrained— grew even faster than the computer empire. Eventually, when the enormity of the debacle became obvious in the boardroom, the computer man was sent on his way—usually to greener users if not pastures—and another was brought in to tidy things up.

John Hoskyns, head of one of Britain's largest software and computer consulting firms, said to the *Economist* in 1970:

> I was talking to someone in a large American user company in New York recently, where they had a project which was originally budgeted for $300,000 in development costs. It has currently cost them $3 million. It shows no signs, in fact, of being completed, and they have managed to get through eight top data processing vice-presidents in seven years. I talked to number nine, and he was not in very good shape.

Since Hoskyns talked to the *Economist*, number ten has taken over.

Isolation may, in fact, be the largest problem of all. Not only have company managers and computer industry people isolated themselves from each other, but computer people even within a single company tend to ignore each other. One company has 25 profit centers and 25 computer centers. It also has 25 different kinds of programs for such common applications as payroll or invoicing. None of them is interchangeable.

Another communications chasm was also reaching Grand Canyon proportions. Not only were the computer makers and users falling further out of touch, but the computer academics increasingly retired to their isolated towers, coming out only to deliver abstruse papers to each other at elite colloquiums. Instead of training students to go out into the industrial world and make computers do sensible work, they grew more research oriented, spurred on by aerospace and government grants in the United States. Thus, they simply created more academics in their own images. This situation is likely to continue until more industry people infiltrate academic gatherings and the universities themselves with down-to-earth reports of industry's needs—or until more academics go out and spend their sabbatical years doing nonresearch inside companies.

The computer salesmen went blithely on selling their wares to new users and trying to ignore the complaints of old ones—complaints, in their view, being the responsibility of the installation people or the software people, not the sales people.

A situation like this could not go on, accelerating as the industry mushroomed. Entire subindustries grew up to fill the gap between the computer people and the end users. As software got more complicated, specialists set up shop (and eventually body shop) to write the special instructions that each computer needed in a different form to do an actual job for a company.

Most companies do not like to admit publicly that they have spent money foolishly. Their stockholders, customers, and employees expect an image of wisdom and achievement. Even so, users began banding together and quietly voicing dissatisfaction with their soaring costs, first in user groups attached to the various computer manufacturers, then in industry associations and occasionally at computer conferences. Once the level of complaint grew from a murmur to a wail, the hitherto inviolate manufacturers found themselves standing somewhat nakedly with their latest-generation finery, like the emperor who thought he was going out in elegant new clothes.

Chief executives began demanding clearer answers to their questions: How much has it cost? How much *will* it cost? How much will it save? What reason do we have to believe it can be done within that estimate? Do we really need it? Are there other ways of getting the job done?

They began getting answers too. It has become more obvious in recent years that a noncomputer man with administrative skills is perfectly able to learn enough about what computers do to do a good job of managing one. A computer man with excellent technical skills today, on the other hand, may have a much harder time learning how to manage people and allocate the resources that are absorbed in data processing. These can no longer be limitless.

The next step from the user's point of view will be the creation of an "information director," who is responsible not so much for the computer as for the sensible flow of information throughout the company and for the use of the latest sensible techniques for using that information in the context of the business. This requires first of all a *manager,* then some grounding in data processing, data communications, operations research, organization and methods, and information theory.

Organization structure in computing is one thing. The organizational structure in the corporation is much more important. When you hire a director of MIS (or an Information Director, or whatever you want to call him), you are in the centralization business, according to Philip Dorn, one of the early members of SHARE (the IBM scientific users' group) and computer adviser to one of the largest companies in the United States.

Dorn points out that the "typical" multidivisional company with $500 million turnover, a number of plants, and a number of product lines has had its computing decentralized in the past, with perhaps seven to fifteen small machines in the 360/20 class, five or six in the 360/30 class, and one or two large ones in the 360/65 class, plus a smattering of older computers and specialized systems. Bringing these together into a few centers is a major task, but if it is carried out properly the individual user departments get more computing at less cost, and the corporation does too. "Centralization doesn't cut costs," says Dorn, "but it helps you hold the line. More important, it gives you technical benefits." He lists common people, programs, purchasing, and policies as major benefits. People can be shifted back and forth between divisions and the central computer centers more easily. It is possible to develop specialization in certain centers that can serve other portions of the corporation. Scientific and administrative people can be treated more uniformly and fairly, and uniform billing policies for machines and people can be developed. "You get fairly good leverage when you go out with one order for the entire corporation, too," Dorn notes.

Figure 1-1 shows Philip Dorn's concept of the optimal corporate structure—from the DP manager's viewpoint. Figure 1-2, from the same view,

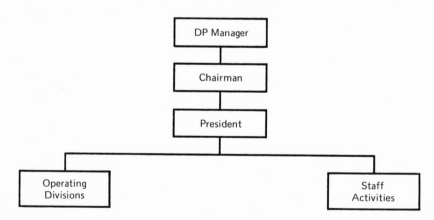

Fig. 1-1. Optimal structure for computing.
Source: DP Managers.

shows the "normal" structure. Figure 1-3 is Dorn's suggestion for a potentially viable structure. "It's not optimal," he comments, "but it could
give you some idea of where you want to be in five years without tearing
the corporation apart."

In all this discussion of centralization, it may be helpful to remember
that the computer, used sensibly with data communications equipment, can
also be a tool in *decentralizing* a company's operations. In either case the
concept of the information director is important.

Most users do not have a $500 million turnover. But even in a small-
to-medium-size company, the information director (by some name) will
more than pay for himself. Whether his function is line or staff, he will
have to be a man of extraordinary tact (and be backed by a strong mandate from the board) to engineer the consent of departments that lose
"their own" computers in a centralization drive.

Centralization can come about most easily in larger companies after
decentralization of computing has raised the level of numeracy or cut the
fear of the computer among managers in operating departments and divisions. One large company that tried to leap directly from feudal paperwork
to the latest cybernetic management system in the mid-sixties lost millions

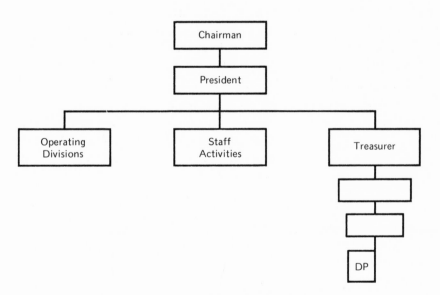

Fig. 1-2. Normal structure for computing.
Source: DP Managers.

as autocratic division leaders refused to attend planning meetings, raised trouble with unions, sabotaged centralization structures, and met every proposal for a central computer with an impassioned counterproposal for a different kind of computer, thus involving an army of computer salesmen in the debacle, which is still going on. Similar strife in other companies tends to be shrouded in secrecy, but the cost is enormous.

The remote terminal offers one polite path to centralization. If a small computer in an operating department can be augmented with communications equipment to allow it to exchange information with a central system, the department often feels it has gained a piece of equipment rather than losing control of one. Many second-generation computers can be so enhanced. If this is not possible, it is usually worth the extra expense to install the new remote terminal next to the old system for a month or two of overlap as programs are shifted onto the central system, while people get used to the new procedures and come to view the new terminal as analogous

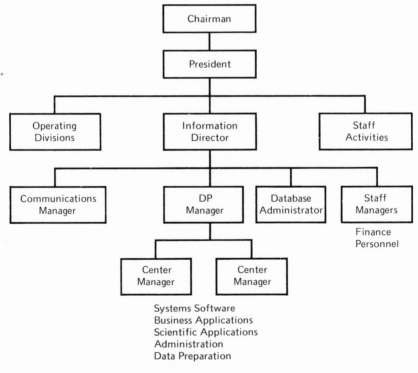

Fig. 1-3. A potential structure for computing.
Source: Philip Dorn.

to the old computer. (Departments that have not previously had computers will not suffer the same emotional bereavement.)

Centralization doesn't mean one single location for a large company. This is neither necessary nor wise, since having backup at another location can help if one center suffers damage or disruption from Acts of God or computer haters. The local computer manager should be fairly autonomous in the things that affect his dealings with his local plant, though overall policies can be set from the corporate headquarters.

THE COSTING CHALLENGE

The information director's first job is to be able to ask and answer the time-honored questions: "What is going on?" and "How much is it costing?" This means in most companies that it is important to get a good financial man before you get a good technical man. Whether he operates in the line manner shown in Figure 1-3 or in a staff capacity, as some consultants suggest, he will need to see data processing costs broken down into reasonable cost centers. Philip Dorn suggests the following simplistic set:

Data Preparation, which includes keypunch operators, devices that operate unattended at night, and all sources of data gathering. Data "gathering" can cost four times as much as mere "source data collection." Very few computer people see where the data originates or what it costs to bring it to the door of the computer center.

Personnel Services, which includes direct charges to user departments for all programming, systems analysis, and consulting time from inside and outside sources.

Computing Services, which are primarily machine time. Some companies bill their users at an ascending rate as they use core storage.

Peripheral Services, which includes the printer, card readers, and tapes and disks, as well as other input/output devices. It also makes sense to bill user departments exponentially as they demand more tapes and disks to be mounted. Peripheral services also include such human tasks as collating work and the mail boys who carry around the tons of paper nobody reads.

Remote Services, which includes the cost of terminals, communications lines, etc. People who deal through remote terminals usually handle their printing and card reading very differently, so these charges should also be separated.

There are major problems in costing any computer services on a reasonable basis, and inequities are inevitable. Should the central computer or the user terminal pay for communications costs, including the people who are hired to spend all their time dealing with the telephone company? How should storage be charged for when a central database is used by remote departments? These charging policies will affect the decisions to buy bigger computers, high-cost/low-use storage, expensive data circuits, and other costly but sometimes useful amendments to the system that no single user department could justify alone.

PROJECT CONTROL AND HIGH-PAYOFF APPLICATIONS

Another key to successful computer use is project control, again a management matter rather than a technical one. Dr. Maurice Kendall, chairman of the Scicon consulting firm in London, puts it this way: "You set up checkpoints at the start of a computer project and say: 'When we reach this point we will have a long, hard look. And not by anyone who is involved in the project.'"

Coordination between departments is a perennial problem; so is management involvement. Too often user departments ignore a project after the feasibility study, until it is time to use the resulting program and they discover facets that don't suit them. One sensible form of project control is to charge user departments for some portion of their development costs. In one company the user department is entirely responsible for getting quotations from the computer department for new projects, comparing these with bureau or software house quotations, then justifying the results to top management.

This charging approach makes sense because the manager with his own budget committed to the project will not only be more cooperative, he will also watch even more carefully than a DP manager to make sure his project develops smoothly. Even so, most veterans agree that it is wise to double every estimate for project development costs, and at the same time slice the projected benefits in half.

Choosing the right things for the computer to do is a top management function in which the information director should eventually have a say. Each company will have its own pattern, but cost-effectiveness should be the general guideline. Air Products, Ltd., in England spends £250,000 per year running its computers, which originally cost about £500,000 for the hardware and £400,000 for the systems and software work. The company's payroll still runs on accounting machines because management believes it would not be profitable to do payroll on a computer. The computers are used instead to forecast demand for industrial gases and to schedule production and distribution, using linear programming techniques. Thus Air Products has a working plan every Thursday for the week ahead, and a tentative plan for the second week ahead, taking into account demand from 10,000 customers, the maximum and minimum production capacity at a number of large plants, existing power tariffs, the number of distribution vehicles available for the 16,000 delivery points, where the excess products are stored within the network of eight cylinder depots, and the minimum stock levels. The work plan is then amended by daily analysis of orders. Most deliveries take place within 24 hours of receiving the orders. The computer also handles the financial details and paperwork for these transactions. Air Products, Ltd., thinks the investment has paid off in higher profits.

It isn't necessary to get a new computer to achieve a higher payoff. Even the most antique installation can benefit from better management controls in the computer room. Standards for operators, for example, can save thousands every month. One company found that some operators were taking four times as long as others to put the computer system into its real-time mode of operation. Simply watching the "wait" light, analyzing the console printouts, and controlling the operation procedures can give a 10 to 25 percent increase in the amount of computer time available for real work.

The British Institute of Management (BIM), assisted by Brandon Applied Research, surveyed 102 companies about their practices and attitudes concerning computers. The results were published in a £5 report called *Achieving Computer Profitability*. BIM found that the vast majority of companies that had installed computers did so primarily to improve management information—a justification that is notoriously difficult to quantify before the fact or to measure afterward. But companies installing their second or subsequent computers were usually doing so for tidying-up reasons: to handle increased work loads, to extend existing systems, to handle additional or more specialized applications, or to speed up operations.

The survey included a question about the future applications that the companies thought would have the greatest payoff. More than half of these experienced companies were already using their computers for inventory control, and this was by far the leading application for future attention as well. Inventory control was followed closely by production planning and control. Other areas that were mentioned included project evaluation, financial and marketing models, control of cash, assessment of opportunity for profit, investment planning, profitability forecasting, modeling and simulation, profit and efficiency reporting, operations research, and decision-making systems. Accounting applications were notably missing from the list!

The primary reasons given for unsuccessful systems (in the eyes of the user companies) were inadequate planning, followed by wrong systems specifications and low-quality systems analysis or programming work.

When it finished analyzing the results of the survey, the British Institute of Management summarized the key management factors that made computer operations more successful:

1. Stop looking at computers and start looking at your business. Don't regard the computer as a panacea for the problems of your organization.
2. Don't rush it. Be prepared to creep, crawl, walk, and run—in that order.
3. Spend as much time as possible on a feasibility study to determine the problems and likely benefits and to establish the priority areas for computer applications.
4. Ensure top management appreciation, interest, backing, and responsibility.
5. Spend plenty of time on training and educating *all* levels of staff. Dispel the myth of the "black box" as early as possible.
6. Make sure you understand the potential user's anxieties and problems. Gain confidence of line managers and staff by early involvement and discussions. The ultimate success of any system depends on good human communication and understanding.
7. Recruit first-class DP people—some internally, if possible.
8. Recruit a DP *manager*, not a technician. Make sure he has adequate status within the organization.
9. Don't underestimate the time and costs involved in developing systems and programs.
10. Analyze systems and potential applications to make sure that the databases are reliable and comprehensive.
11. Keep systems as simple as possible.
12. Lay down standards for systems, programming, and operating.

2

Dealing with the
Computer Makers

The mainframe (or computer, or "central processor") in a computer system is simply the engine. If you didn't have it, you wouldn't go. The mainframe horsepower can range from minimodels to racing number-crunchers. No matter how good the motor, if it's not kept in good repair, you still won't run with any peace of mind.

Neither a dent in the bumper nor a pothole in the road is sufficient reason to go out and buy a new engine for your car. (If you insist on driving a new Cadillac every year for aesthetic, comfort, or social reasons, the luxury clearly justifies itself—as a luxury— in your framework of values.) Usually a good mechanic or a set of driving lessons will go a long way toward improving the car's usefulness. So it is with computers.

This book is not a tome on the internal combustion of computers—though it might be mentioned here that the innards of a few recent models have been shown to be highly flammable. In this chapter we shall dispense with the mainframe—a superfast moron—once and for all. It is more important to know about the range of services that can save the expense of hyperfast morons, and make existing fast morons a little brighter.

THE JARGON

Technically, a computer consists of four fundamental parts: one that adds chunks of zeros and ones very rapidly—the arithmetic or *central processing unit* (CPU); one that holds them in temporary or permanent form—the *memory*; one that shunts them around—the *input/output system*; and one that acts as a policeman, roadmap, and mastermind for the others—the *control unit*, which is normally located with the CPU.

The central processor does its job by storing the *bits* (binary digits—zeros and ones, in other words) in its *registers.* A register is an electronic gadget that holds a number of the bits until the controller tells it to add another set of bits to the existing set and send the result somewhere else. The bits are arranged in sets of six (called *characters*) or eight (called *bytes*), usually with extra bits appended to check that they have been sent back and forth properly. The characters or bytes are then arranged in computer *words*, which can carry anything from 16 to 48 or more bits of information in addition to the checking bits.

Every computer manufacturer will extol the virtues of his own particular arrangement of bits, bytes, words, registers, and how they interact. For the average manager, this is totally unimportant, except that the arrangement in one system should be easy to fit together with the arrangement in another system. (They rarely are.) This computer "architecture" is seldom as important as your own file architecture—the way the company's information is arranged in its files, whether they be card files or computer files.

The storage system in a computer can hold mountains of files, billions of bits. The faster you want to find the information in memory and get it into the CPU, the more you have to pay for the storage system. The fastest and most expensive kind of storage is usually *core.* Normal core storage systems hold from a few thousand to about half a million computer words. One million words of core will soon be practical.

Cycle time is a term the computer manufacturers use to tell how long it takes to go into core, find a word, and bring it out into a register. Cycle times around one millionth of a second (one microsecond) are common. In modern computers, however, cycle times are much less important than the *throughput,* the actual amount of work the entire system can do in a specified time. This is a matter of how all the parts of the system are arranged, whether they can all do useful work at one time, and how reliable they all are. Nanosecond or picosecond cycle times don't do you any good if the system is constantly down because of an unreliable $500 typewriter. One of the fastest computers in machine throughput actually has ten small, rather old-fashioned CPUs with slow cycle times working together under a clever controller. This concept is called *multiprocessing.*

Next after core store in descending price order comes magnetic *disk storage*. A group of disks like very fine phonograph records are stacked in such a way that small moving heads can reach each part of each disk. Access times are normally 30 to 60 thousandths of a second (milliseconds). Disk systems hold up to 50 or 100 million words fairly comfortably. Capacities up to 500 million words will be common in a few years.

For faster retrieval there are the fixed-head (magnetic drum) storage systems, which can hold more than 11 million bytes and take about 2.5 milliseconds to retrieve one of them. Magnetic tape can hold up to 20 million bytes on a 2400-foot reel, but it usually takes several minutes to find a particular word even on the fastest systems.

Punched cards are probably the most commonly used storage medium, and one of the cheapest for moderate amounts of information that is used regularly and doesn't change very much. A single card holds 80 letters or numbers. Small computer systems can sometimes store programs and data on punched paper tape. This is more prevalent in economy-minded European countries than it is in America. It's messy, but it's cheap, and it works.

The input/output (I/O) system consists of the channels inside the computer system, the "ports" through which the information flows, the wires or telephone lines that carry it, and any auxiliary processors, front ends, or other devices that help squeeze it, stretch it, or push it along. The I/O system also includes all the devices at the ends of the wires or phone lines that originate or receive information. The most common devices (or *peripherals*) are:

- card readers and punches
- paper tape readers and punches
- typewriter-like devices, some with television screens called CRT (cathode ray tube) or VDU (video display unit) terminals in the acronymic way of computer people
- magnetic tape readers
- auxiliary disk systems, some with portable disk packs
- line printers

Most of these are electromechanical monsters that work in macro-seconds rather than microseconds and have a fiendish tendency to break down at critical moments. They cost far more than they should, and are generally the Achilles' heel of the computer system.

Computer systems can generally be described as *I/O-bound,* which simply means the central processor spends entirely too much time waiting for the peripherals to act before it can get on with its other tasks.

The controller is the brains of the electronic brain. This is a combination of electronic gadgetry (hardware) and complicated and very clever codes for guidance (software) that keeps everything else moving. If you type in a request to add 2 + 2, the controller must first send out to one location in storage where it directs the system to send back a byte that contains 00000010 and put it in a register in the CPU. Then the controller sends out to another location for another byte that contains 00000010 and puts it in the register, which flops over so that it contains 00000100. The controller then sends the result to yet another location. Then it tells the I/O system to translate the byte from binary into decimal and print out a "4" on your terminal. The process gets very complicated. If the human being who must in the end tell the superfast moron what to do happens to skip a step or leave out a comma, errors of alarming magnitude can occur. A human being would not turn out a $1 million check for a $100 invoice, but he might fail to instruct the computer how to do it properly. The computer does not make mistakes—it only follows orders.

Each computer has 100 or so elemental hardware *instructions* (with such names as "Add A to B" or "Jump to B if Greater Than"), which give it its unique personality. These hardware instructions are full of fancy logic, and therefore quite expensive to make, so their number is kept to a minimum. But the arrangement and choice of instructions make it easier for certain computers to do certain kinds of jobs. Thus a machine that has hardware instructions for handling decimal information easily or shifting long strings of bytes around in chunks (rather than one-at-a-time) is better suited to banks or insurance companies than one that has hardware instructions for finding square roots or multiplying by pi. Each manufacturer presently has a different instruction set for each computer model, though quite a few have instruction sets that are similar enough to IBM's 360 series so that they can entice users with the promise of low change-over cost.

Several computers (including IBM's own 360 and 370) have *emulators* for earlier popular computers like the IBM 1401—or for current competitors. These are microprogrammed (relatively untouchable hardware/software hybrids) to work as if the new computer had the hardware instructions of the old. Eventually it will be possible to plug in emulators to copy the latest rather than the earliest machines. Computer manufacturers don't like to talk about this; they are all vulnerable to emulation.

The present computer systems are arranged so they run in batch mode, or real-time mode, or time-sharing mode, or various other modes, with rather cumbersome setting-up and changeover procedures from mode to mode. Eventually a "user-mode" machine may appear if enough people demand it. This would shift more rapidly and without cluttering up the operation with different procedures (and jargon) for each mode.

Unless you are addicted to technology, the human and political facets of the computer industry are much more pertinent. The next time a computer salesman starts bandying around phrases like "terminal-oriented software with multiprogramming capability for three-dimensional users," simply ask him why the computers that are being delivered today are the ones that salesmen were promising ten years ago.

Dr. Herbert Grosch from the U.S. National Bureau of Standards is sometimes regarded as the Ralph Nader of the computer industry. He condemns computer manufacturers for purposeful complication of their systems, masking the relative simplicity (and elegance) of the hardware by overcomplicated and often unsuitable software. Dr. Grosch is also the originator of the term "Snow White and the Seven (minus n) Dwarfs" to describe the computer manufacturers.

THE COMPUTER MAKERS

Snow White is, of course, IBM, which has exercised a fairly benign worldwide domination of the industry since its inception. The dwarfs used to include General Electric (GE), Honeywell, Control Data Corporation (CDC), Univac, Burroughs, RCA, Digital Equipment Corporation (DEC), National Cash Register (NCR), and Xerox Data Systems (XDS). By late 1971 Honeywell had bought out GE's computer interests; RCA had noisily thrown in the towel, then sold its customer base to Univac; Digital had taken a step toward large computers but reverted to the safety of its smaller models; and there were signs that NCR would revert to sophisticated accounting machines as quietly as possible. Xerox blended XDS into the corporate entity, with plans to tie computers more closely to copiers over telephone lines. In Europe, Britain's ICL is the largest computer maker (and has held IBM to less than half the British computer market, with some government encouragement). Others are CII in France, Siemens and AEG-Telefunken in Germany, Philips in Holland (plus other companies in other countries that make minicomputers or specialized computers), and a touch of Olivetti in Italy, though Olivetti sold its computer interests to GE (now Honeywell) a number of years ago, and now concentrates on terminals.

There's a lot of action and interaction among the computer makers, enough to make many users wary when they commit themselves to non-IBM equipment. Therefore, they watch every move closely. So far, neither GE nor RCA customers have suffered withdrawal of support, but users are more alert to the danger. Careful review of IBM's own support policies when it decides to do away with an old product might give more comfort to those who feel particularly exposed with Spectra 70 installations.

IBM's domination (between 70 and 80 percent of the worldwide computer market) has forced the smaller firms to amalgamate, cooperate, and cross-license each other's products in order to concentrate their limited research and development funds on selected specialties. To put it simply, Univac and Control Data are particularly noted for their huge remote-access computers, developed first for solving scientific problems but now rather useful for large companies or bureaus. CDC continues to prefer the scientific market, but Univac is bringing out medium-size communications-oriented computers for the business market, and also hopes to keep 15 to 30 percent of the 360-compatible users it bought from RCA. NCR and DEC concentrate their resources on smaller machines; NCR's, in particular, tend to be designed for accounting types of applications. (NCR and CDC have a joint company now to design future computers.) Burroughs makes rather elegant machines for research and is also working hard for a share of the difficult banking market. XDS was one of the earliest contenders for the medium-sized scientific market as well as time-sharing hardware. Philips makes a range of relatively small office computers, as do other European companies such as Nixdorf and Regnecentralen. Scratch an ICL graphics terminal and you'll find a CDC nameplate. Similarly, ICL sells peripherals to Friden, CDC, Burroughs, and any other computer maker that wants them. CDC, Burroughs, NCR, and Univac also furnish various peripherals to most of the others on cross-license arrangements.

In 1970 ICL teamed with CDC and CII to create a Belgium-based company called Multinational Data. The purpose of this venture was to advance work in standards, by which equipment from one manufacturer could more cheaply and easily be plugged into a system from another. This means that all the "interfaces" or places where peripherals, computer hardware, and computer software join each other should be identical—a

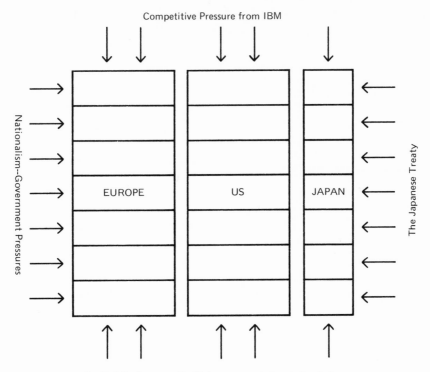

Fig. 2-1.

laudable goal and one that has absorbed more energy than the fourteenth-century alchemists spent looking for a way to change lead into gold. Other manufacturers will support Multinational Data if it makes visible progress. They have to, in an IBM-dominated world. But in late 1971 ICL opted out of a joint CDC-CII venture to develop a new range of IBM-compatible computers, so worldwide standardization may come through some other medium than Multinational Data, although it began to publish standards in 1972.

UNBUNDLING

No matter how standardized a dozen other computer makers can make their products, the real standards in the computer industry come from IBM. Equipment is "360-compatible" or a terminal is a "2780-type."

A disk is 10 percent less expensive than "the comparable 2314" or "3330."

IBM's pricing policies also set the de facto standards. Until 1970 these prices had been relatively high, high enough for competitors to flourish and low enough for people to go on buying computers. The delicate balance between responsibility to users, the industry, and the stockholders was impeccably maintained by the company, which had grown to almost a quarter of a million employees, a turnover of about $7 billion annually, and profits around $1 billion.

This kind of responsibility is difficult to maintain in a large company, but IBM did a fair job. One apocryphal story concerns an enthusiastic young software expert who found a way to cut out several steps in software that was frequently used by IBM customers. The savings in a typical installation from this small change amounted to about 4 percent improvement. It was later calculated that by delaying the need for new systems for these users, he had cost IBM about $12 million in revenue.

The word *bundling* comes from an ages-old custom in chilly climates. Young couples were tucked into bed to do their courting with a bolster or "bundling board" between them for propriety. In April 1969, just as the economic climate was beginning to look chillier, IBM made its famous unbundling announcement, which threw the computer industry into confusion and consternation. (Since then, the other manufacturers have been trying to hop into each other's bed.) Until that time, certain software and services that were necessary to most users had been bundled in with the price of the basic computer system. These extras included not only the "systems software" that made the computers run but also the compilers that gave them their languages, the applications programs that did most standardized jobs, the courses that taught how to use the hardware and software, the maintenance of the machines, and the "systems engineering" help to design new systems and make existing systems do new tasks.

IBM didn't achieve 70 percent or so of the world market for computers without an acute instinct for trends. Realizing that there was a growing market for these software and service elements of the systems, IBM announced that its computers would be sold after a certain date (which varied from one country to another as IBM deemed best) with separate charges for some of the previously included software and services. In the United States the prices of some hardware items were dropped 3 to 5 percent to compensate. Elsewhere they were not changed. The applications software (Program Products, in IBM language) in particular became extra. So did systems engineering and most courses, though here too exceptions were negotiated.

To competitors and users alike, it was as if a gentle Saint Bernard had suddenly started nipping her pups. The announcement set off a rash of policy announcements from all the other computer makers, most of whom settled down to modified forms of unbundling as it suited their markets.

The effect of IBM's unbundling on users was not a noticeable drop in charges. Support costs for the average installation went up by about 10 to 15 percent. The announcement did, however, give impetus to a fledgling computer education industry, and to a few large software companies that were beginning to bid for large contracts with "systems engineering" content, in which the software company rather than the computer company could take full responsibility for putting together the equipment and programs to do a specific job.

Unbundling had surprisingly little effect on the sale of "packaged" software, off-the-shelf programs for specific applications, which were still moving more slowly than had been predicted. The full effects throughout the hardware and software portions of the industry did not take hold until the 370 series began to be delivered in 1971.

Whether the effects of the recession contributed or not is a moot point, but most users did not use as many services (from IBM or anyone else) as they had before extra charges were imposed. Large companies that already had systems analysts and programmers simply used their own resources to greater effect. More cooperation took place within industry associations and local government groups, which banded together with more reason to share software or develop their own videotaped training courses. Some users deferred new projects or found they could do without. For a number of users, unbundling made no immediate difference to the cost of computing. For most, it pushed them into attitudes of greater independence.

One major effect of the unbundling decision was the sudden difficulty users found in evaluating computer bids. Instead of a single standard contract form, the U.S. government found itself with six or seven, with separate negotiations for the maintenance and other support services. To translate the different quotations of four manufacturers into something that could be compared and ranked became a task worthy of a separate computer of its own.

Unbundling gave a boost to another segment of the population—the legal profession. Some user companies began to need a full-time lawyer just to analyze new computer contracts. The patent situation for computerized applications is still murky. Then there were the new lawsuits.

Computer leasing companies, software houses, peripheral companies, users, even the U.S. Department of Justice began suing IBM (at an increasing rate as several of the first lawsuits were settled out of court for large sums). IBM hired a former attorney general of the United States and began filing some lawsuits of its own, which cut down the rate of new contenders. The lawsuits took two basic forms. If IBM introduced a new program or service without charge to existing users, people who were already selling such a program or service filed antitrust suits, charging that IBM was trying to hog their markets. If IBM began charging for something that had previously been included, such customers as the leasing companies complained that IBM was trying to take over *their* corner of the market. By late 1971 IBM was reputed to be spending about $200 million a year on legal expenses alone.

THE LATEST GENERATION

With the increased clamor from users that their systems have been a disappointment, and the noise of unbundling and lawsuits within the industry, few people have noticed that the latest generation of computer hardware announced by the manufacturers in 1970 and 1971 is very good indeed from a design viewpoint. It also saves users quite a bit of money.

Most computer people identify the generations of computers by their components. Relays and vacuum tubes characterized the cumbersome first generation, giving way to discrete transistors in the second, and microcircuits of one sort or another in the third. There are enough new twists on componentry now that claims for next-generation technology simply add confusion, not clarity.

A much more useful historical breakdown concerns the way computers are used. The first machines, based on the Von Neumann concept, did one task at a time, with the memory, I/O, and arithmetic built in with the controller. In the second generation, the memory, arithmetic, and I/O were separated somewhat, but the controller could only deal with one of them at a time (called *synchronous* operation), based on a rigorous internal clock. Finally, asynchronous input/output was possible, which permitted more than one program to run at a time. Coupled systems, in which several controllers had access to a single memory, for example, developed because they gave extra redundancy for critical "real-time" operations, especially in the aerospace business. From there it was an evolutionary step to coupling different parts of different systems at different times through phone lines. Coupling the hardware for these systems was challenging, but writing the software was overwhelming. Some of the time-sharing software promised in 1966 has still not been delivered in proper working order.

Most of the machines announced in 1970 and 1971 actually do the things that were claimed for the third-generation machines. In fact they are capable of doing far more, but people are still learning to do third-generation tasks. Although it is unbelievably complicated by now (and has cost the manufacturers a fortune), the software with few exceptions can handle a number of users doing different work, so long as they observe a fairly strict protocol. Most of the systems work over telephone lines fairly reliably—more reliably than the telephone lines themselves transmit the information. Most of IBM's Program Products (and everyone else's) actually do the jobs they were designed for. Furthermore, most of these new-generation machines cost about the same as their predecessors, but can do up to 50 percent more useful work for the money.

Briefly, the manufacturers announced the following new computer families in 1970 and 1971 (for delivery in 1971-73):

IBM	370 series (370/135, 370/145, etc.)
Univac	1106, 1110, and improvements to 9000 series
Burroughs	700 series (1700, 5700, etc.)
Honeywell	2000 series and 6000 series (6030, 6040, etc.)
CDC	STAR-100 and improvements to 6000 series
ICL	1900S series (1901S, 1902S, etc.)
Xerox	improvements to Sigma series (mostly software)
DEC	DECsystem 10 and small PDP models

With respect to size (taking the IBM 360/65 as a "large" machine), these a̠ ͜ generally large machines. STAR-100 is a huge thing, with many little processors for research applications. Univac's 1110 is even bigger than its already large 1108 and 1106, but the 9700 announced late in 1971 moves the Univac product line down toward the normal-size business user. Honeywell's 6000 series builds on its large 600 series (inherited from GE). The Sigma 9 is an agglomeration of Sigma 7s, which were already large. Much of the Burroughs series is in this class too, as are the 370/155 and 370/165. ICL chose to keep its enhancements in the medium-size range, with a new range held back for 1972-73.

Most of these are "multiprocessors," computers that have more than one central processing unit. Most of them are also suited (by software and control mechanisms) to "multiprogramming," which means that more than one program can run at a time. Multiprogramming, in practical terms, gives considerably higher payoff than running a nonmultiprogramming computer for an extra shift per day.

At the other end of the spectrum are the minicomputers. Many of the modern minis have all the memory, I/O, software, and sophistication of the million-dollar models of the mid-sixties. The minis are generally available for $10,000 to $25,000. Because the major computer manufacturers show little inclination to cut prices and complexity overnight, there is a growing underground movement to replace large computers in commercial environments with clusters of minicomputers, dispersed according to the needs of the company. If each one were dedicated to a single task, and accessed by a separate telephone number from user terminals, it would be possible to do away with the excessively complicated and expensive software that giant systems need to flop users in and out of the computer (like wet fish). Without software, you have less bugs. If something does go wrong with a mini in a cluster, you can plug in a spare. The idea is seductive and will certainly gain ground in some kinds of applications. For one thing, with the exception of DEC, none of the big mini manufacturers is also a big computer manufacturer; therefore, they are not hamstrung by the technology-oriented attitudes that have grown up within the computer industry.

As the computer generations passed, an absurd situation came into being. Far too many of the fast new machines were being run as if they were first-generation machines or even card-sorting equipment. As a company got a new machine, it simply took the old procedures and translated them. From cards to a 1401, from the 1401 to a 360/30, from there to a 370/135, still working in "1401-emulator mode." Manufacturers have had little incentive to help customers tidy up the programs as they transferred—the slower they ran, the sooner the customer would need another computer. The users themselves have been so busy coping with crises that getting a program to work at all on the new system was a major achievement. Few companies involved in a generation change could afford the time to go back to the user department, discuss the new machine and its capabilities, and explore new ways of getting the job done, or whether it needed doing in the same form at all.

Similarly, old reports may or may not be useful, but they are familiar, and give managers a sense of security. So most DP managers try to create exactly the same reports on the new system, as much for reassurance as for expedience. The same slovenly tendency holds for "data." One insurance company in New York buys about one million cards a month for its computer. It destroys about half a million. The difference, which would fill an average-size office cubicle from floor to ceiling, dissolves into hundreds of file cabinets and storerooms throughout the 60-story headquarters. But slowly, someday, the saturation point will be reached, and the insurance company will need another 60-story building "for expansion." Healthy growth is quite a different matter from adding adipose tissue.

In some computer rooms, the arrival of new-generation machines brought to the surface some of these problems and led to healthy slimming programs and retraining or reorganization. The majority of people working in existing computer installations were not up to date on multiprogramming or the latest nuances of languages. Many were fearful that the new systems would demand new skills, though others welcomed the challenge.

These workable new mainframes may indeed be the *last* computer generation for a while—perhaps they should be. A single U.S. user spent over $6.5 million just converting programs from second- to third-generation computers. With the onset of recessions in the United States and Europe, computer purchases slowed rather drastically, and this has cut into research budgets for the computer manufacturers. A five-year or even ten-year hiatus, while users catch up with the already existing generations and learn to use them well, would benefit everybody and give the manufacturers a clearer mandate for their future generations.

STANDARDIZATION

The strongest mandate is going to be for standard interconnections that let any devices use any software on any computer. Computer users (by which I mean top management—not computer professionals—in companies that use computers) must carry some of the blame for the standardization mess that exists today. They have dodged a real responsibility because they were too busy or too awed. The manufacturers are even guiltier. For two decades they have oversold the benefits of their computers and blithely ignored the consequences. (In several computer companies the leading salesmen used to earn more than the president.) They have dominated the industry and dictated its directions. They have also resisted most attempts at standardization, and anything else that would make it easier for users to take programs written for one brand of computer and run them on another.

Dr. Herbert Grosch, known for his outspoken views on standardization, suggests that there are three levels of compatibility that users need. At the lowest level is compatibility of media, such as recording standards for magnetic tape, physical properties, codes for magnetic and paper tape, the layouts of keyboards, and such things. Here, he thinks that progress is hampered by the vested interests of the various manufacturers.

Dr. Grosch's next level for standardization is computer languages. He blames not only the manufacturers for lack of progress here but also the computer professionals, who are held back by their pride and prejudices.

His third level of compatibility concerns standard "packages" that can be plugged into various computers with almost no special programming to do specific jobs. The lack of advance here, in Dr. Grosch's view, is partly due to the isolationist views of top management, who prefer to think that each of their own precious applications is too special and individual to be done by a standard package.

Eventually market pressure (the cumulative effect of individual demands) could conceivably bring about machines that are truly interchangeable, as well as special languages for each industry or application—languages that could work on any machine. Technically this is feasible, but human inertia will probably keep it in the realm of wishful thinking, unless accounting concepts, with respect to computer-related activities, change drastically—to reveal to more managers the true cost of their nonstandard computing ways.

There are hardware, software, or firmware approaches to this challenge. The machinery and instructions in a computer are growing so complicated and intertwined that it gets more difficult to sort them out. Eventually many things that are software today can be plugged into the new computers as physical cards, with new forms of storage holding the instructions permanently (so long as the firmware is plugged in), which means they work fast and efficiently like hardware instructions, but are changeable like software instructions. This means a special language or program could be literally plugged in to make the computer an optimum machine for accounting; then the firmware could be replaced by a general timesharing language that restored the machine to design engineers and management information uses.

One of the earliest approaches to standardization involved software. A universal machine-independent language was proposed that would translate all languages for all machines. A more recent proposal is a complete turnaround—that all computers be furnished with a universal language based on identical instruction sets, from which all other languages could be built. This idea is not likely to appeal to computer makers, particularly IBM, which would retain existing customers by making it more difficult, not easier, to transfer programs from one machine to another—unless it be a more expensive machine from the same manufacturer. This feature is called *upward compatibility* and appears in most computer brochures and presentations.

The ideal approach, of course, is the least likely to gain acceptance, because it would be opposed by users (as well as manufacturers) threatened with eventual change. Nonetheless, if computer manufacturers were forced to produce universal-language machines at the most basic instruction-set level, they would then compete at the firmware level, not at the level of wired logic or at the high level of programming language. This would not only provide a real solution to the compatibility problem, it would also allow the manufacturers to concentrate their research and development money where it belongs—in applications. If IBM could spend a healthy percentage of the money it has invested in PL/1 (a language that is supposed to be all things to all users) on firmware for production control and manufacturing applications, the credibility and usefulness of computers would be singularly improved. Similarly, DEC's machines for the printing industry, Burroughs' university and bank computers, Control Data's aerospace number-crunchers could all be specialized and optimized at a lower level that extended their usefulness and efficiency. This might eliminate the average applications programmer as we know him today, by allowing him to be an industry specialist instead of a computer specialist. It would also be extremely helpful for the development of one-off systems; and in basic computer research a firmware development could lead to hardware state-of-the-art improvement when it had been completely explored and proven.

New circuit techniques (which may or may not appear under a "new generation" label) will be available before 1975 to make firmware economically attractive. Already the manufacturers themselves are using firmware in several ways in their present computers—including emulating each other. A few users have also created their own additions to instruction sets by ordering "empty" emulators (rather cumbersome devices that normally contain the instruction sets of the previous generation of computers). A skilled technical team can fill the empty emulator with its own choice of instructions. Allen-Babcock Company, a Los Angeles bureau, created 25 instructions that optimized its third-generation computer for PL/1 time-sharing service, with particular attention to list processing and floating decimal operations. This helped the computer run 50 percent more work than competitive bureaus could handle on similar machines.

At first glance, standardization seems to be a constricting thing, fitting every computer and every user into the same size and shape of straitjacket. This is certainly how the majority of computer manufacturers view it; the efforts so far have come from end-user groups, sometimes including representatives of governments who view themselves primarily as users rather than regulating bodies. These people, and we hope more as companies grow more mature in their use of computers, view standardization—*at the right levels*—as a series of steps that can free them rather than inhibit them, by eliminating unnecessary differences and complexities. This could free capable people to pay more attention to the unique problems of each organization that could be handled effectively if the computer were treated as a tool rather than an expensive toy.

3

Plugging-In Periphery

When you buy a car you also choose the optional gadgets and accessories that suit your own tastes. Extra mirrors outside, a radio, a heater, an extra carburetor, leather seats. Or you can add some of these to your existing car if you decide to keep it for another few years. You don't have to visit your car dealer to get most of these "extras." The nearest garage will suffice.

The peripherals in a computer system are analogous not only to these accessories, but also to the wheels of the car. Without some of them, you can't move, no matter how good the engine. Like tires, some are considerably more reliable than others, and worth the extra cost.

Changing to larger wheels on a car is a fairly major mechanical task. Changing to faster peripherals on a computer system can be not only a mechanical challenge but also an electronic one. Even so, the peripheral manufacturers have made considerable progress in this area, generally by making their devices "plug-to-plug" compatible with comparable IBM devices. The user who knows what he is doing can take a stripped-down IBM 360 mainframe, tuck in a large core store from Ampex, plug in disks from Data Devices, and add a communications front-end from Interdata to handle terminals from Teletype, Ferranti, GTE, and Sanders, while his Data Products line printer and Potter tape drives work efficiently at the computer center. (These names are examples rather than recommendations.)

This raises an appalling jurisdictional situation. Envisage a disaster in which the leased mainframe goes down along with a disk drive, while a card reader has clogged itself, and in the resulting chaos someone spills coffee into the line printer (one reason coffee doesn't belong in the computer room). Who is responsible for tidying up the mess? The leasing company calls in IBM, which says the disk was improperly connected. The disk man doesn't have any inclination to explore the mainframe. A line printer repairman points out that his company's contract specifically absolves it from responsibility for coffee damage, while the card people say you've been using inferior cards.

It is seldom this grim all at once, but some peripherals are more intimately connected to the mainframe than others. Even though a mixed system can save quite a bit of money, it may bring more headaches than it's worth unless you clarify responsibilities and develop enough maintenance ability in-house to avoid the worst of the wrangling.

THE GREAT PERIPHERAL PRICE WAR

Computer manufacturers in general and IBM in particular frown on mixed systems, though their own high-cost peripherals historically have helped the trend along. When the latest intergeneration computers were announced, a number of users, instead of trading upward, traded in their older computers for stripped-down new ones and began adding their own peripherals. The result was a slight drop in their monthly payments to the computer manufacturers, who had envisaged selling more power, but not at less revenue.

IBM in particular must tread very carefully when it is competing with smaller fellows in the peripheral field. Direct aggression or corporate policies that forbade non-IBM peripherals would draw instant antitrust action from the U.S. government, though for many years, IBM (like the telephone company), was able to insist on the use of its own peripherals "to protect the mainframe." IBM gave way only as the tape and disk manufacturers were able to prove laboriously that their equipment met the same technical standards.

In the memory field, IBM began to initiate lawsuits against companies that had hired key technical people. The IBM research laboratories are known as the "happy hunting ground" among peripheral-equipment manufacturers. Many other graduates of the giant company go into business for themselves after they have reached a certain plateau within IBM's hierarchy. Other manufacturers have also spawned clusters of independent offshoots, specializing in making a single product or range of products at a lower price.

IBM also fought back with price cuts on some older peripherals, which naturally forced similar action among other manufacturers. More frequently, the devices were introduced with new features and new model numbers to mask the price change or soften its effect. Finally, as a finite number of disk systems in particular seemed to be going to the independents just as the recession took effect, IBM brought out new disk systems at considerably lower cost, but took care to locate the controllers *inside* the 370 CPU itself. When the controller is bundled with the mainframe, it is decidedly harder to make and sell a cheaper disk system.

Peripherals are still overpriced, underreliable, and the limiting factor on most computer systems. They tend to be bulky, awkward, electro-mechanical elephants compared with the elegant, sleek mainframes. Nonetheless, they are improving rapidly, and will continue to do so. For this reason, even if you are currently blessed with a single-manufacturer system or are contemplating one, it would be wise to make sure you are technically and contractually free to add or substitute cost-effective peripherals whenever they become available at a sufficiently attractive price. Shopping around costs a little time but can be made fairly painless by willing peripheral salesmen. It also gives a sensible basis for negotiating with the manufacturers themselves who have some room for price adjustments whenever there is "systems work" (or special interconnection) involved in a larger configuration. If you can get the same device at the same price from the mainframe company, your life will be simpler when it comes to maintenance.

A quick summary of the various peripheral devices and their most common features may be helpful. Detailed lists of the devices, their prices, and their manufacturers in the United States are published (and updated regularly) in *Datamation Industry Digest*.[1] Full-scale evaluations of various classes of peripherals are available from Auerbach.[2]

1. *Datamation Industry Digest* is available from *Datamation* magazine, at 94 South Los Robles Street, Pasadena, California 91101. The digest costs $25 in the United States and $35 overseas.

2. A notebook of peripheral equipment descriptions and evaluations is available from Auerbach Publishers Inc., 121 North Broad Street, Philadelphia, Pennsylvania 19107.

DISK SYSTEMS

A disk system is the fastest and now the most commonly used storage medium for programs and frequently used data on third-generation computer systems. It is less often used with older computers, simply because the controlling software for the mainframe (its "operating system") must be written differently when information is shunting back and forth from disks at a rapid rate. It is possible to use quite a small third-generation computer with a desk-drawer disk system. Many are available on a turn-key basis (see Chapter 9) for data collection, in-house time sharing, school applications, or other specific industrial or accounting uses.

Although they are not as common as shredded wheat, disk drives lead the peripheral pack when it comes to using IBM's own numbers to identify speed, size, and other characteristics. Most other disk makers have model-numbering systems that give instant clues to their IBM counterparts.

The disks themselves are analogous to phonograph records, only much more delicate and expensive. They come in single units or multiple stacks, either fixed permanently in the disk drive or removable as "disk-packs." A disk drive handles a single record or stack, and the controller can usually manage a number of drives working at the same time.

One of IBM's earliest successful disk models was the 2311 system, which held a little over 7 million bytes of information on a removable disk-pack. Average access time was about 75 milliseconds. Even more popular now is the 2314 model, which has up to eight drives per controller. Average access time for the 2314 is about 60 milliseconds.

The old IBM 2321 "datacell" was really an array of magnetic strips that were picked up and wrapped on a drum. Access times ranged from 125 to 600 milliseconds.

In IBM's new model 3330 disk system (which is already attracting imitators), the controller can handle up to eight drives. The drives come in pairs and each drive can hold up to 100 million bytes on its 19 recording surfaces, with 30-millisecond average access time.

Disk systems are subject to appalling disasters because a bad disk can ruin its drive, and a bad drive can wipe out its disks and all their data in an instant. Less than alert operators "testing" bad disks on other drives or new disks on a suspect drive can compound a disaster rapidly. All manufacturers provide their disks and drives with elaborate instructions for care and handling, which should be followed to the letter. When a drive crashes, it can take hours or days to repair and bring it back onto the crippled system. When a disk-pack is wiped out, it costs not only the replacement pack but also the time and effort to restore all the lost data—if the job can be done at all.

MAGNETIC TAPES

Magnetic tape is one of the most commonly used storage media for programs and data, especially with older computer systems. Even on systems that also have disks, tape is a sensible and less expensive way of storing historical data and programs that are run infrequently. A reel of tape that can hold up to 20 million bytes of information requires only a couple of inches of shelf space.

Advances in tape technology have concentrated on improving the speed with which the tape drives can search for and retrieve information and on cramming more and more information onto a tape. The ultimate bible-on-the-head-of-a-pin system, already in commercial existence, uses a laser rather than a magnetic tape recorder to blaze tiny pinpricks several hundred deep on a special coating of a half-inch wide tape, jamming them equally compactly along the length of the tape so that the 300,000 or so tapes the U.S. government keeps in its archives could be compressed onto less than 300 of the laser tapes. A smaller, weaker laser is then used to read back the information, at a speed that conforms to tape drive technology. However, retrieval is usually faster because the desired information is less likely to be 2400 feet away at the other end of the tape.

The normal, nonlaser tape system runs the tape past the reading head at up to 200 inches per second when it is looking for information, and stores each byte as a 7-bit or 9-bit set of impulses (6 or 8 for information plus a checking bit) along the tape. These are normally spread out along the tape at 556 or 800 bits per inch (bpi), though some of the newest systems are able to use 1600-bpi densities.

Tapes do not react kindly to heavy-handed treatment. They are also vulnerable to sabotage by a disgruntled employee with a magnet. Their edges tatter rather easily, which causes information to be lost. A slightly bent tape reel can cause havoc to the entire 2400-foot thread of information. Again, the manufacturers' instructions for handling are worthy of attention. If the information is worth storing, it is worth protecting.

More than one installation has invested in dual-density (556 and 800 bits per inch) tape systems, but only uses the lower density, probably because earlier tapes existed already at that density. A few adjustments to file-handling software and some programs may be worth the effort if the faster capability (already paid for with the tape drives) can be used. Not only can more tape programs be run, but the computer also spends less of its time waiting as information flows in from the tapes.

Another new development that will eventually be important in industrial computing is Ampex's so-called terabit memory, in which information is recorded very densely onto videotape. Like the laser memory from Precision Instruments and other new mass storage media (such as experimental holographic systems that can re-create the entire "picture" of the data even when part of it has been damaged), the terabit system was originally designed for scientific users, notably in the oil and aerospace industries, which are voracious consumers of storage.

Magnetic tape cassettes, similar to those used for home music systems, are also coming into vogue, especially for capturing data from typewriter-like terminals. These can accept data very slowly, then be read into the computer (local or remote) or fed onto high-speed tape in batches, to be processed in the evening when the normal load is lighter. Because the tape is sealed into its cassette, it is better suited for handling by an untrained staff than by a large tape reel.

CARD EQUIPMENT

Punched cards preceded the electronic computer, and will still be around when the computer has changed almost beyond recognition. The cards are bulky, easy to get out of order, and difficult for machines to handle without damage at high speed. They are also familiar, comforting, visible, and readable by human beings when sufficiently motivated. When it automated its payroll system with punched time cards, one computer company encountered strangely high numbers of programmers who threatened to resign unless their salaries were increased to some magic sum they deduced that some other programmer received. No matter how often the company changed the pay codes, they were decoded. The phenomenon disappeared only when the pay codes were entirely eliminated from the cards, at considerable expense.

Speeds have increased somewhat, but the card reader and punch today are surprisingly similar to their counterparts ten years ago. For what they do, they are also surprisingly expensive and unreliable. Card readers tend to react neurotically to bent cards, incomplete punching, or a change in the weather. Very few readers or punches are normally able to run at their rated speeds, no matter what the manufacturers say. Speeds for readers range from 600 to 1200 cards per minute; punches operate from 120 to 300 cards per minute.

Smaller, slower card readers for remote use are beginning to be available at lower prices. Some of these have made significant advances on the reliability front, though there is still room for improvement.

The cheapest card punch of all is perhaps IBM's Port-A-Punch, which has been sold to schools for about $7 each so that children can prepare their own programs at home, using the card holder with a special stylus. Several clever classes have produced their own models, somewhat more delicate to punch properly, for a few cents apiece.

PAPER TAPE

Paper tape with five or eight holes punched across it is a natural by-product of the old-fashioned Teletype, which is today the most commonly used time-sharing terminal. Paper tape is also a useful medium for writing and storing short programs at the computer center, especially in smaller installations. The faster paper tape readers today can handle up to 1000 characters per second.

For many users, paper tape is much less expensive than cassettes for transactions such as invoicing that are recorded one-at-a-time on forms in a teletypewriter and simultaneously on the tape. The paper tapes can be read into the computer at full speed (usually a dreary and noisy ten characters per second) from the paper tape reader that is built into the Teletype. They can also be checked for errors first and corrected before they are transmitted. The savings in equipment may evaporate in telephone charges and computer time at this speed, but for small or remote offices the ability to produce the written record and the computer input simultaneously, without changing procedures, may be quite convenient. The tapes are easy to handle and identify—the common pencil or magic marker on the leader can resolve the problem of the mysterious 4-foot length somebody found in the corner cabinet. Tapes can also be stored in anything from a thread box to a desk drawer, and the readers are fairly tolerant with old, scruffy tapes. To make changes or corrections on a paper tape, you can punch "delete" and "insert" marks on the old one, which will skip or stop as necessary when you use it to produce a newer, cleaner copy.

Paper tape "chad," the confettilike holes that are punched out of the paper, is very convenient for New Year's Eve and Guy Fawkes Day celebrations, but otherwise a nuisance in the average office, where it can clog the Teletype itself and any nearby office machines unless a proper covered chad-collector is used religiously.

LINE PRINTERS

The impressive line printer, spitting out its reams of forms and reports, is the often inadequate funnel through which most of the computer's output flows. A large computer can be brought almost to a complete standstill if there aren't enough paths for the information flowing out. One hardware analysis group studied a number of systems and reported that they were in the wait state about 80 percent of the time, with some of the banks of memory used less than one percent of the time— which makes the computer a rather expensive printer-controller. In such situations the expense of an additional printer or a small computer to control line printers can bring savings in computer time alone, not to mention the pacifying effect on users waiting for their jobs.

Line printers are measured and priced by their speed, which is counted in lines per minute (lpm). Like card equipment, they seldom run at the full rated speed. IBM's rated line printer speeds run from 600 to 2000 lpm. Such features as uppercase and lowercase characters are rather expensively available.

As with card readers, a few remote (and seemingly reliable) line printers are beginning to come on the market from the independent manufacturers. These tend to run at 300 or 600 lpm. Many are incorporated as part of remote batch terminals.

VOICE AND CHARACTER INPUT/OUTPUT

Most business communications take the form of human conversations or letters and forms. Computer people have been notoriously unsuccessful in their attempts to use these directly for input, though major advances are coming during the seventies.

Optical mark readers are already available at high but not quite outrageous prices; they have been in use for many years for reading examination papers and other forms that can be encoded with a pencil or pen. Most of the current models no longer require special pencils, and many can differentiate between lighter and darker marks, selecting the darkest in any group. Filling out such a form can be a laborious process unless the information is in simple yes/no or choice-of-five format.

Hand-printed or even typed information is considerably more difficult. There is a direct relationship between the variety of letters that can be read and the cost of the reader. The device must not only find a bar or mark and identify its location, it must also relate it to many other marks, and decide whether this square A and that triangular A are the same letter, or whether the square one is really a B with the bottom line drawn lightly. The locations and styles of hand-printed letters also vary from one writer to another. Typewriters have such a plethora of typefaces and type sizes, too, that even this much standardization is difficult. Several typefaces have been developed and attempts made to standardize them for optical character readers (OCRs), but the one the machines read most easily is awkward for human beings, and the one human beings prefer is still less than 100 percent reliable for the OCRs. One compromise that seems to be gaining ground internationally is called OCR-B.

A clever hybrid device with some of the advantages of mark readers as well as character readers is now available for about $10,000. This is a remote terminal (that is, it can send its information through telephone lines to a computer located elsewhere), based on input from a simple golf-ball typewriter. A special golf ball prints normal letters with small bar codes beneath each letter, so the human beings can immediately see a readable text that seems generally underscored, while the mark reader sees sensible input codes and ignores the extraneous matter floating above them.

On the voice input side, there is an even sharper relationship between the size of vocabulary a voice-reader can recognize and the cost of the device. Voice recognition systems that know a few words are already on the market, and can be used for certain kinds of reports or requests from salesmen in the field, but these systems seldom justify their cost. Each voice varies so much in its inflections, timbre, and pronunciations that technologists have followed the science-fiction writers into a search for a voice-print machine that would be even more accurate than fingerprinting. It is still a long time before the average executive can dictate his letters or reports directly into a voice-reader for computerized handling.

On the output side, line printers and terminals are already spitting out typed matter, sometimes in upper- and lower-case letters that are perfectly adequate for office use. The importance of this feature has been underestimated by computer people for years, which may have retarded the use of computers in practical business applications. Several companies brought financial forecasting software packages onto the market in 1968. One package (Foresight) specified that the time-sharing program should be used only with a particular type of terminal that prints like a normal typewriter. The end users, who were financial men and general managers rather than computer people, responded warmly to the familiar-looking typed reports, in business English and a commonly accepted format. As a result, Foresight gained an advantage for several years, even over programs that did more sophisticated calculations.

Like upper- and lower-case terminals, or voice and character input devices, voice output devices cost more according to the vocabulary size. A number of practical systems already on the market have several hundred words of vocabulary. These usually work from the computer center over telephone lines. Coded requests for information can be sent from any telephone, using lightweight and inexpensive pushbutton terminals, with answers returned directly by voice. These systems are expected to improve rapidly. As more pushbutton phones come into use, using specific tones for specific numbers and combinations of tones for letters, the terminal costs will drop still further.

MICROINFORMATION AND COM

Most people are accustomed to getting their information on the typed or printed page, a bulky, easily misplaced medium, but rather popular ever since Gutenberg printed the first Bible.

In recent years, computer output onto microfilm (COM) has made it possible to store hundreds or thousands of pages of information in a very small space, and find them again as easily as looking something up in a book. This is done in several ways, and the output is available in several forms. All of them involve photographic processing.

To make these "microforms" (the generic name for any kind of microfilmed material), the computer either creates a printout that is automatically photographed, or it causes miniature letters and numbers to be captured directly on the film. Very sophisticated (and thus expensive) film-setters have more choices of type sizes and typefaces than the average high-class printer, and films from these machines are often used for printing directories and other widely distributed but frequently changing kinds of information. The information is not fed to them directly from the computer, but through an intermediate medium, normally magnetic tape.

For much lower costs, books, articles, almost any paper of any size can be captured on microfilm (which comes in a roll like any other film), or mounted on microfiche (which arranges dozens of pages in each direction on a pocketbook-size slide). These microfiches or microfilms are then slipped into relatively inexpensive viewers (often under $200) that magnify the tiny images and present the reader with a larger-than-life-size page image. With several thousand pages per microfiche, retrieved easily by moving the card until a marker points to the desired number, it is possible to carry an entire library in a shoebox. Microfiche also costs considerably less than paper to print. National Aeronautics and Space Administration documents in the United States are published for about $3.00 in paperback or 65 cents on microfiche.

Hill, Samuel & Company, Ltd., the London banking firm, is using microfiche and microfilm for its share registration service. Certain information about share transactions is required by law to be available to the public and to be accurate within a month. The full registers are thus stored on microfilm, but they are accessed rather rarely. On the other hand, Hill Samuel and its clients need more up-to-date information for day-to-day office use. This amounts to "immediate access to noncurrent information," a common need in business, but one that is seldom recognized by computer people. To do the same job with on-line terminals would cost a great deal, but unless the information were updated in real time (which is *not* a common need in business, even though it has become fashionable), no advantage would be gained. Nor is there any advantage in storing the information on a disk. All of Hill Samuel's files are held on magnetic tape, by far the cheapest medium for this volume. The COM system produces a weekly microfiche that is distributed widely for coding and all other routine clerical functions, with a summary register every week for every company. Because they hold 6000 accounts each, a mere 350 microfiche cards replace all the preceding visible register cards. These are accessed about 400,000 times a year, which would be extremely expensive in phone charges alone for an on-line system.

COMMUNICATIONS MYSTERIES

The telephone has already figured largely in descriptions of peripheral devices. The line printer, the card reader, and voice or character equipment commonly work over telephone lines. This doesn't happen just by magic. Something must translate the vocal or mechanical or electrical impulse coming into the system into a form that can be carried across the telephone lines, then translated again when it reaches the computer center into the on/off electrical impulses that the computer recognizes. The same thing happens in reverse when the computer is sending information to the terminal.

This means there must be special equipment at each end of the line. Some computers can be purchased with such equipment from the manufacturer, but so many companies have specialized in the data communications equipment field that it is worthwhile to shop around.

At the computer end of the system, there is a communications controller or "front-end" that accepts the remote inputs. IBM is again the standard setter, and independent offerings are often numbered according to IBM's 2701, 2702, and 2703 communications gear for the 360 series and 2703 for the 370 computers. Some of the newer front-ends or communications computers are programmable, which means a change in the computer, terminal, speed, or language specifications can be accommodated simply by changing the program in the front end.

At the remote end there are many choices of equipment for data communications, according to the type and speed of the terminal, line printer, or other device. Most of these are available from the telephone company. Some are available *only* from the telephone company. In Britain it still costs £8 per month from the post office, which will eventually give way to commercial suppliers. The most commonly used communications device at the terminal end for smaller terminals is a "modem," which in the United States can be purchased outright for as little as $100.

"Modem" stands for "modulate-demodulate," which simply means it changes (or modulates) the terminal's impulses into tones, and vice versa. The same process occurs through another modem at the computer center. You can hear the tones harmoniously zipping along the lines if you eavesdrop on a modem. (This is, incidentally, rather easy to do. If your people commonly send highly confidential information to a computer over such terminals, it may be worth exploring the value of scrambling and unscrambling equipment at both ends of the line.)

Between the terminal and the computer, more elaborate networks (such as those created for bureaus—see Chapter 11) have a bewildering variety of words for the small computers or devices that shunt the traffic around or collect it in larger chunks and speed it up to save money on telephone charges. These include:

> *concentrators,* which concentrate a number of input lines onto one line and pack their information more tightly
>
> *multiplexors,* which mix the incoming lines onto a single line, and do the squeezing as well, though less often
>
> *communications computers,* which can multiplex or concentrate at network nodes, or serve as front ends at the computer center, or both
>
> *store-and-forward computers,* which can hold onto the information from a terminal or computer until a central computer or another terminal asks for it

If you remember only two things about these devices, you will be able to stay out of trouble. First, a "programmable" concentrator or multiplexor (one based on a small computer) that can be changed as the system changes is usually worth the extra cost. Most systems *do* change, and rightly so, as new devices or communications facilities become available, or as company needs change.

Second, if you are going to install a network with data communications, make sure you have a first-class communications man of your own, rather than depending on the services of the equipment purveyors or the telephone company. (The telephone company, incidentally, is a good place to go headhunting for your own first-class communications man.) Then, when troubles arrive, your own people are better equipped to diagnose whether a problem originated in the central computer, the high-speed lines, the local exchange, the concentrator, or the connection at the user's end. Your own communications wizard will also be able to phone an old friend at the correct office in the mysterious depths of the telephone company, saying: "George, we've got a bad circuit out of Minneapolis," rather than filling in forms and going through the agonies of information starvation while the telephone company sends out the wrong sort of specialist to solve what it thinks might be the problem at the computer center in Chicago. You are also less likely to get into jurisdictional disputes. Telephone maintenance people are just like computer maintenance people when it comes to blaming the other fellow's gear. Only another telephone man can know enough of the nuances of the equipment and the jargon to sidestep these wrangles.

Another practical policy is to take the telephone company into your confidence at the very earliest stages of planning a network. Your data communications system is absolutely dependent on telephone facilities. Exchanges at different places have different equipment, different levels of saturation, and different types of skilled staff (or shortages thereof). If you locate your network nodes in places that make it easier for the telephone company to accommodate you, you will obviously get better service. There is also a chronic and worldwide shortage of leased lines, the faster private telephone lines that make data communications more reliable and practical. The more advance notice you can give the telecommunications people, the more likely you are to get your lines more or less on time. This holds true even at the earliest planning stages; knowing your plans can help the telephone company plan its own production and network improvements.

In the United States several 1971 decisions by the Federal Communications Commission have opened the doors for independent companies to offer special services for data communications. These are often cheaper than comparable Bell System facilities, and their existence has spurred Bell on to some advanced data networking of its own. Again, if you can do your shopping around at the earliest planning stages, before network locations are frozen, you will have a better chance of getting good facilities on time, whether from the independents or the telephone companies.

THE UBIQUITOUS TERMINAL

A "terminal" can be anything from a $200 device in a salesman's briefcase, which sends a few coded reports from a pay telephone, to a $200,000 conglomeration of computer, line printer, card reader, television, and more esoteric additions, still working over a telephone to another computer somewhere else. Even so, various classes of terminals have their own uses and characteristics.

One of the cheapest terminals for time sharing (see Chapter 11) is the teletypewriter, which costs approximately $900 in full communications dress. The common Telex can also be used as a time-sharing terminal to some bureaus, with no additional charge for the terminal if you are already a subscriber to the Telex network.

Somewhat more expensive with communications gear is the type-writer terminal, which has normal typefaces (and interchangeable "golf balls" for those based on IBM's model 2741 terminal). When you see the term "full ASCII character set" in a terminal advertisement, the alphabet soup refers to the 128 uppercase and lowercase letters, numbers, symbols, and control codes that are specified by the American National Standards Institute coding convention (as opposed to the "EBCDIC" coding convention, which IBM preferred for many years). These codes are important to the computer too because the job of translating them into machine language is different in different computers. There are also ASCII subsets for 96 characters (uppercase and lowercase with fewer symbols and control codes) or 64 characters (uppercase only).

"CRT or VDU terminals" (cathode ray tubes—as in television screens—or visual display units) are simply typewriter terminals that also have television-type screens. They usually display printing as white-on-black or green-on-black. The readability of the characters varies considerably, but not always in relation to the price. The more expensive models usually have more storage built-in, which can cut down on line charges and make it easier to edit inputs before they are sent to the computer.

Early enthusiasts (and a few current ones) suggested that the chief executive of a company should have a snazzy CRT on his desk, from which he could request any information he wanted about his company and get instant answers on his screen. This MIS (management information system) myth fell into disrepute when it was oversold before the realities of systems analysis and software had been realized. The questions in the sixties had to be rigidly formatted, and so did the information in files, so the top manager had to specify the few types of questions he was likely to want to ask, and a few years later he might be able to ask half of them, but no others. With tortoiselike rapidity, this situation is improving (see Chapter 6). IBM itself has a workable management information system based on one of the world's finest information-gathering devices: the telephone. The IBM managers telephone their requests to human beings in the information room. These people look up the requested information in paper files, microfiche files, or computer files; they put it into the desired order and format; then they telephone it back or send it by means of a mailboy on old-fashioned paper.

The cheapest CRT terminals now cost less than $3000, and prices have not yet settled down to their eventual levels. They vary according to the number of characters the terminal can display; 512 and 1024 are common, though a few CRTs have full-size pages analogous to the printed page. Some have built-in storage (called a "buffer") that can hold up to 5000 characters, which means that you can either split the screen into two to four pages, or flip or roll continuously through the few pages that are stored locally. This is convenient and can save computer charges because the display is maintained (or "refreshed") from the local storage instead of being retransmitted every few milliseconds from the central computer. The buffer also permits the user to write information and display it on the screen locally, then change, correct, or update it before he transmits it to the computer for storage or processing. The convenience of the editing also affects the price (and usefulness) of a CRT. A movable marker called the "cursor" shows where you are, and in some systems it moves more flexibly and sensibly than in others. Sometimes lines or words can be inserted or deleted, and the terminal will automatically adjust (or even justify) the rest of the text. Some keyboards are arranged for data collection, often with portions of the display that the operator is unable to change. Others are built for commercial time-sharing services and have special symbols for mathematical operations.

One advance in CRT terminals, long overdue but beginning to look practical, is called "hard copy." This is the ability to make paper copies of the information on the screen. The earliest hard copy systems were just Polaroid cameras, which made copies that could be deciphered with some measure of squinting. More recently electrostatic copiers (similar to the ubiquitous Xerox) have been connected to terminals so they capture the electronic impulses going to the screen and make black-on-white copies when the user presses a button. These take a few seconds each, usually more for the first copy of a display. Although they still cost a few thousand dollars, the technology is improving rapidly and prices will drop sharply during the seventies.

"Intelligent" terminals come in all sizes from high-IQ CRTs to full-scale remote-batch terminal computers. These are simply programmable (and therefore changeable) computers that have enough storage built-in to do some jobs locally, and to adapt to the different formats and requirements of several kinds of large computers at the other end of the line. Because this adaptability is dependent on software provided by the manufacturer with his intelligent terminal, make sure which computers it matches before you invest, and leave room for future flexibility by insisting that software will be furnished automatically as it is developed for new central computers. Terminals with a modicum of intelligence are available in the $10,000 region, but most of them cost more and do more.

The full-scale remote-batch terminal is classically a small computer (the source of the intelligence), a line printer, a card reader, and a keyboard, with or without CRT. Prices start around $20,000. An existing second-generation or third-generation computer of the 1130 or 360/20 class makes a first-class remote-batch terminal by the addition of communications gear and appropriate software, without requiring people to familiarize themselves with an entire conglomeration of new equipment. In every case, the remote-batch terminal needs the right software to communicate with the central computer.

Data input terminals are a proliferating class by themselves. These usually work in clusters with their own small central computer and storage system (disks or tapes or both), replacing old-fashioned keypunches or collecting data from new sources with varying degrees of economic merit. They have varying capabilities for local verifying and editing—the mildly intelligent models needed for future data gathering have been called "disciplined" terminals to differentiate them from the highly intelligent, flexible, and powerful models used for remote-batch. These terminals are much more dependent on the emotional reactions of their operators than is at first evident—which makes training ease and human engineering important selection criteria. The reactions of keypunch supervisors should also be an important factor in choosing a data input system. Most of these terminals have keyboards arranged like the old keypunches, sometimes with separate numerical keys. Many display the information on a CRT as it is punched, so operators can see mistakes more easily; this may be an expensive luxury for most users. Some have changeable formats, which can be imposed from their own processors, making sure that the inputs go into the correct fields in the file (or the form, as it appears on a screen).

Shop-floor terminals have been developed to read information from employee badges or time cards and job cards or other shop-floor documentation. These are expensive and often cumbersome, but improving rapidly. Special terminals for computer-aided design are also dropping in price, but still justify specialist consultants and often need their own dedicated computers. Yet other special-purpose terminals are on the way, for salesmen or route drivers, for typing and invoicing classified advertisements, for blind programmers, for handling inventory control and general accounting. Prices are still dropping here, too, and pioneering can be expensive, but the terminals bear watching.

SHOPPING AROUND

With such an awesome list of peripherals available from so many different suppliers, the typical user reacts by trying to keep an up-to-date database on prices and characteristics. This is expensive and unnecessary because several companies are already doing just that on a service basis.

It is much less expensive to pay for an off-the-shelf evaluation of a certain class of peripherals when you decide there may be a need for new equipment. A few telephone calls to leading suppliers will bring eager salesmen with additional information. After the first flush of familiarization, it may be more rewarding to send out a questionnaire listing your desired characteristics than to sit through another round of presentations. Be sure to include a question about which other companies in your area or industry are already using the equipment. Then follow up the references. They will probably provide your most helpful and unbiased evaluation inputs. Ask particularly about the quality of maintenance and training, especially when equipment is furnished by entrepreneurial new companies. If you are buying large volumes of terminals, ask to have a few demonstrators and use them for several weeks (most time-sharing companies welcome even short-term customers) so you learn their weaknesses as well as their benefits.

Financing mixed systems can be an arduous task. Computer leasing companies generally prefer to stick with IBM equipment or at least the first-rank computer manufacturers, where the market for second-hand equipment (and thus their risk) is known. If you absolutely cannot run your business without the first ten production models from the Widget OCR Corporation, you had better be prepared to tie up your own capital. You might also want to keep some in reserve for next year, when Widget runs out of development money and threatens to go bankrupt with your ten devices 90 percent finished. This kind of pioneering leads to instant diversification almost as fast as the in-house/out-house computer bureau.

Peripherals call for a corporate lawyer or contracts man who understands the computer business almost as much as mainframes do. Businesslike negotiations and clear contracts will take some of the perils out of mixed systems, and give you time to worry about the important things—like why the chairman lost his yacht race last weekend, using the new sails designed by the CAD department, when the chief systems analyst spent two days and tied up the only line printer for three hours while figuring out an optimum course.

4

Working with Consultants

Let us leave the bright realm of visible hardware, with its quantifiable characteristics and fixed or negotiable price tags, and look at the mysterious services and software that can have a much sharper effect on the profitability of a company as well as its computer.

Over the lifetime of a car you deal with a number of specialists: the maintenance men at the dealer's garage; the wizard at the body shop who eased the dents out of the bumper after that little contretemps at the traffic light; the more dubious expert who fixes the heater every six weeks; the one who fills the tank every week; and (if you're lucky) a trustworthy mechanic/magician who tunes it up, does its periodic checkups, and tells you when you need special work done. If you maintain a fleet of autos, it may be worthwhile to have a chief magician and a few specialists on the payroll. But for most drivers, these services are needed only intermittently, so the experts remain on someone else's payroll. You pay a surcharge as a result, and you can't always be sure of getting the best mechanic when you go to a new garage, but it costs less overall.

The designers and maintenance men who can create a computer system and keep it well tuned cover an even wider spectrum. They can be specialists, hired for the most abstruse technical tasks, or generalists, retained to bring a sense of balance and an expert outside view to the overall organization, not just its computers. They may be individuals, working from their kitchen tables, or organizations with hundreds of employees. The contract may be for a week or for ten man-years. Neither the degree of specialization nor the size of the organization should mask the fact that you are putting your system or parts of it into the hands of human beings, and are depending on them to hand you back a better system.

WORKING DEFINITION

A consultant is an outsider you bring in to do a specific job. You are renting his experience and objectivity. No more, no less. The better you specify the job to be done, the more satisfied you are likely to be with the consultant's work. That's why it is important to make sure his understanding of the specification matches your own. This can extend all the way to: "Come in and have a look at this mess and tell me what I ought to be specifying for consultants or my own people to do about it." This can be a perfectly reasonable consulting specification at the strategic level; it happens fairly often, though it is seldom stated this clearly.

A 1970 study of the problems and attitudes of 400 data processing managers and executives in the United States showed that 83 percent needed outside help in upgrading technical knowledge in their organizations; 49 percent had no documented plan for developing their installations over the next few years; of those who did have plans, almost 50 percent had not been approved by top management; 32 percent had not even identified applications to be implemented in the next two to three years; more than 33 percent reported their staff turnover to be above 20 percent per year; 72 percent plan to use outside service companies to help solve their problems.

It is interesting to note that they refer to "outside service companies" rather than consultants. Except for the large, established consulting firms, the word suffered from overuse in the United States, particularly as recession set in in 1969 and 1970. Every unemployed programmer or systems analyst tended to call himself a "consultant" until he could find permanent employment again. During this era a gruff DP manager growled his own paraphrase of George Bernard Shaw's maxim: "Those who can, do; those who can't, consult." Another retorted with the definition: "A consultant is a liar from out of town with a briefcase."

The smaller British consultants and consulting companies have had less trouble keeping their images polished and establishing professional relationships such as those of accountants, attorneys, or doctors with their clients or patients. There seems to be a subtle social inversion as one crosses the Atlantic—possibly related to relative earnings. In Britain people tend to say "my accountant" in the same reverent tones Americans reserve for "my doctor." Conversely, the average British doctor seems as overworked and underpaid as the average American in-house accountant. It is also interesting that the most expensive medical specialists in Britain are called "consultants." So are a few topflight U.S. corporate accountants.

In New York, Newcastle, or New Guinea, an ongoing though intermittent professional relationship is the one most likely to be fruitful. Holman Hunt, director of management sciences (and computer consulting) for PA Management Consultants in London once commented: "The mark of a bad job at the strategic level is long periods of continuing consulting. When we have done good work, our clients are able to do much more of the task themselves. This means a spasmodic but continuing relationship. Then when we are called back every few years, it is usually to help in breaking new ground."

FROM FEASIBILITY TO FIRE-FIGHTING

Hunt points out that people use consultants only because it pays them in terms of practical results. Other leading consultants echo his point that the most effective use of consultants comes not because the company is "in a mess" or lacks confidence in its ability to solve a particular problem but because it does not choose to have all the relevant experience required to devise and implement the best solution to a problem. If you *are* in a mess, try to bring in help early enough so that the consultant has some chance to improve matters.

Deciding when to call in a consultant is just like any other make-or-buy decision. There are certain advantages:

> *concentration*—A consultant can concentrate on the specific project without being diverted by the day-to-day problems that interrupt other managers.
>
> *experience*—He is retained for his pertinent experience in solving the particular problem at hand. (Unless your problem is absolutely unique, the consultant should be hired for this previous experience rather than his brilliant intellect.)
>
> *impartiality*—His independence lets him make judgments based on facts alone, unaffected by individual interests or internal factions.

In particular, he should have no vested interest in the sale of any particular items of hardware or software.

limited engagement—By hiring a consultant, you can afford a better man than you could spare to the problem from inside. He can leave as soon as the job is finished, so you're not stuck with left-over experts looking for nonexistent problems to solve.

There are disadvantages if you call in a consultant to do ongoing tasks that are properly the function of the company. There are also disadvantages if you keep your people remote from the consultant. You will be wasting an opportunity to expand their knowledge, and giving the consultant less information about the company.

The creation of a computer system or even an individual application usually entails five major phases: first the feasibility study, then planning, design, installation, and operation. Once the system is installed these don't stop; instead they tend to overlap and spread out with the introduction of new applications, new peripherals, new computers, or new organizational structures until the phases are very hard to separate out again into their tidy segments. There are places for the sensible use of consultants in all five phases, depending on the level of specialization the company has brought in-house.

Even before the feasibility study or planning phases it may be worthwhile investing in a management consultant to get outside insight regarding where the computer should fit within the organization and which major areas are most suited to computerization. In most companies there seems to be an inverse relationship between the degree of innovation and the degree of success of an application. Thus, even though some esoteric shop-floor control systems would have a high payoff, at least on paper, it might be more sensible to start on a more mundane level. It is also wise to make sure the system won't slow down your invoicing group while it speeds up payments to your suppliers.

The feasibility study is carried out at this stage to take an unbiased look at whether or not the use of a computer is really justified. The feasibility study leads to a blueprint for the planning and implementation if justification exists. For this reason, a careful feasibility study is probably the most important single step in the process. It is difficult to carry out without the help of an experienced consultant. The manufacturers are biased in favor of large collections of hardware. Too often an in-house feasibility study is, in truth, just a justification exercise. A computer specialist who is to be the future data processing manager is too closely involved and has too much incentive (like the manufacturer) to make a case for a large computer. On the other hand, the in-house computer professional should certainly be working closely with the consultant at the feasibility study stage. Even for a large application, the in-company people often have biases that are too strong to let them consider all the alternatives rationally. Once a procedure for applications feasibility studies is developed and adhered to, the consultant becomes more of a luxury. Such a procedure is described in detail in the following chapter.

Like feasibility, the planning phase can be easier if you use consultants who have experience with similar companies installing systems for similar reasons. The computer manufacturers themselves can be encouraged to offer free consultants at this stage. These are likely to be exceptionally good men, and are worth listening to, though there is little question as to whose equipment they will recommend. In the planning stage you are still concerned with the overall system and how it will fit you.

The design stage is more concerned with selecting the equipment and designing the software to do the job. This also must take into account support, maintenance, standby, and other manufacturer-furnished services. Consultants usually have a wider experience with the different computer manufacturers than does the average user company. Systems are getting complicated enough so that it is often worthwhile having a specialist to make accurate estimates of the system's predicted performance and throughput, simulating its operation if necessary to make sure you have enough computer (or communications) hardware to handle the jobs that have to be done, but not so much that you must go out and sell the leftover 100 hours a week.

At this stage, the consultants from the manufacturers (called "the systems people") can be very helpful with detailed proposals in response to your specifications for the system (which often benefit from the assistance of a specification specialist). Software specs are just as crucial to eventual success, but much harder to establish and measure against. It is important to make sure these are not developed in some remote vacuum separate from the systems and hardware specs.

So far we've had the management consultant, the feasibility studier, the systems man, the simulation expert, and the spec specialist—and we're not even using a computer yet. (A bureau consultant might be called in to advise which one to use in the interim, but that's going a little far. Most companies should be able to make such decisions for themselves.)

Implementation brings a veritable army, if you choose to use them.

You may wish to procure some parts of the system already dressed in software as well as hardware. These are often called "turnkey systems," though they tend to be subsystems. The turnkey company relationship (see Chapter 9) may be analogous to a consultant relationship; unless you are buying an off-the-shelf application, the turnkey people must understand your business as well as their own specialty in order to satisfy you.

If you're installing a mixed system, with pieces from different manufacturers, you will either need a first-class systems company to oversee it all, a first-class team of your own that covers project control, contracts, risk assessment, programming and other specialties, or you'll need people like this on a consulting basis. Unless you are buying a turnkey system or negotiating a "systems contract," you cannot hand over complete responsibility to the consultants for the resulting system. How well it evolves and eventually works is the product of too many internal factors as well as the quality of the planning, design, or implementation stages. "Whose fault?" arguments can be awfully expensive and are generally fruitless unless a systems contract has teeth.

Implementation also marks the most intense period of software development. In addition to the software spec specialist, you could have the documentation expert, control software consultants, applications specialists to take the manufacturer-furnished programs and tailor them to your own procedures, others to write original applications or tailor software packages purchased elsewhere, and yet others to evaluate the results and control the projects.

Programming is not just a matter of sending people on programming courses. It usually takes from six months to a year to reach a useful level of programming proficiency. During ths time the outside specialist can give experienced guidance to your developing programmers. Consultant programmers can also be used to help with overload situations until your own programmer neophytes build up their productivity.

Remembering the mark of a good consulting job, you should be able to expect some of your own people to take over some of these functions by the time the system is implemented.

Once it is up and running, control should certainly rest with the company, not with the clouds of consultants.

At the operating stage, there are still certain tasks in which expert guidance can make a difference. Standards for working the system as well as programming it are a one-time job that is important. Specialists can usually do a better job in many companies than in-house people, who seldom have experience developing standards. The operation phase would also benefit from periodic tuning up from audit specialists, who are really generalists (see Chapter 7).

Selection and training of staff call for different types of specialists. It is often difficult for the corporate personnel man to look beyond beards, brash attitudes, and unconventional dress to differentiate between the superb programmer and the deadbeat. In one California company during the sixties a very senior programmer was hired for a highly technical and secret project. He immediately demanded a couch for his private office, saying he could only work lying down. This was duly delivered, and every time anyone dropped in to see how the project was going he would be so enmeshed in his work that he was difficult to arouse. He was able to get away with his $300-per-week napping for nine months before the first eyebrow was raised. (Project control and personnel screening techniques have both improved since the mid-sixties.)

Specialists in job evaluation can save innumerable headaches. A consulting brochure puts a common problem in perspective: "If I promote Jones, Smith will leave, and if Smith leaves, Brown and Wilson will both expect his job. Whereas Brown can do part of Smith's job, he could do Jones's new job better—then Wilson could have Smith's job. So if I promote Brown, then Jones will leave, and if Jones leaves, Smith won't leave. But who will do Wilson's job? Suppose I promote Jones. . .?"

One warning about personnel consultants: it is awfully easy to pay a fortune and get embroiled in overtesting. This is one way both the company and the consultant like to pass the buck in an area that calls for intuitive judgments. An expert in selection and testing once advised that if anyone offers you a bank of tests that includes Rorschach inkblot analyses, show him the door immediately. These are tools for clinical diagnosis and treatment, not job screening. Similarly, the "free tests" for you or other managers, to "prove the merit of the system," will show you to be a fine fellow with above-average worries and responsibilities. They have about as much pertinence as a Chinese fortune cookie. The same specialist administered sample tests to a room full of personnel men, collected the answers, and returned the next day with confidential profiles for each, in separately marked, sealed envelopes. Nods of sage agreement were visible here and there around the conference room before he revealed that every man had received an identical "analysis."

HOW TO CHOOSE A CONSULTANT

Choosing a consultant is like choosing a computer. Having decided you have a problem or project that merits outside help, you have to spell it out clearly enough to know what kind of consultant to look for. In other words, you need a specification, even if it's scribbled on the back of an envelope, just to choose someone to *advise* you before the specification stage.

Unless you have already established a satisfactory professional relationship with a firm of consultants that is suited to the task, the process should continue, just like the selection of a computer, with competitive bids from the leading people in the required specialty. References from satisfied clients are always an important criterion, but your project is too important to depend entirely on the haphazard "wife's-friend's-cousin" approach or an encounter at a neighborhood party.

Your specification, be it formal or informal, should spell out what you expect the consultant to deliver. These "deliverables" can be reports, plans, specifications, software, or complete systems. Or they can be man-hours (or man-months) whose use is up to you. The more visible your list of deliverables, the more likely you are to get what you want.

The consultants should be asked to submit firm proposals in response to your specification. These should contain the terms of reference for the job (showing their understanding of your specification and problem), the time that will be required, the fees that will be charged, how and when they are to be paid, expenses (which are generally extra), reporting levels and procedures, and preferably the names of individuals who will be working with you, and their alternates.

The low bid is not necessarily the best one to choose, any more than it is for a computer. Because you are only buying the experience and objectivity of the consultant, each firm should be carefully screened. Consulting prices vary from as low as $100 per day to $500 or more, according to the level of experience and the "level" of the job. The best men are usually worth the extra fees, but there are ways to economize. If a top man is supervising a project, his rate should be lower than it would be if you demand that he carry out the entire task himself.

Look at how long the consulting company has been in business, and what types of assignments have been done for what types of clients. Ask how much of their business is repeat business. Look at the backgrounds of the principal consultants, the general level of experience of the staff, and the specific experience of the individuals who will be assigned to your job. It is not necessary to buy a pig-in-a-poke, even when you work with a large firm of consultants. Make sure you meet the alternate in case your leading consultant breaks his leg tripping over an untidy cable in your computer room.

Unlike hardware, it is perfectly reasonable to get your feet a little wet without making a firm commitment to a consulting firm. This is called a survey, and charges are usually reasonable or nonexistent because the survey is the chief weapon in the consultant's marketing arsenal. A survey that takes two or three days is usually free. For five- to ten-day surveys the consultant usually charges a reasonable fixed price.

Since consulting companies seldom advertise, the first-time user may have trouble finding one through any but the wife's-friend's-cousin channels. But computing and management consulting professional groups or trade associations can give general guidance and lists of consulting companies, though they should not be asked for individual references. Groups such as the Association for Computing Machinery in New York City or the British Computer Society in London have codes of professional ethics and can also act as ombudsmen or arbiters in contractual disputes that involve complicated technical matters.

The management consulting associations have stringent codes of professional conduct and standards for entry that assure, for example, that 80 percent of the consultants in British member firms have the equivalent of university degrees, and that firms have been in existence for at least five years. Such conditions are excellent for general consulting, but somewhat unrealistic in the volatile computer industry, where staff turnover is particularly high—though they offer some protection against fly-by-night consulting companies. Consultant turnover is also a criterion in Britain, though it may be a shortsighted one. One leading think-tank in the United States quietly encourages its bright young men to find homes with clients after two or three years with the consulting firm. It believes that the turnover will be high anyway, and the perspective of the client companies and the young professionals will be improved by the cross-fertilization. The company itself also benefits by a growing roster of well-placed alumni and a constant inflow of new blood from the graduate schools. This system works rather well, because a few old-timers are retained at all costs to give continuity and balance to the consulting teams.

Headhunting among your consultant's people is not exactly polite. But it is much less harmful than your consultant headhunting among *your* people. If you encounter this rare absurdity, you are perfectly justified to question his basic business judgment and show him the door immediately.

CONSULTING AND CONTRACTS

In any contract for a large project there are bound to be different points of view between the consultant and his client. These can often be resolved by improving communication—best carried out around a table, with each side presenting its preferred solution or statement of the problem.

A consultant with an objective view, even if it differs from yours, is doing the job you hired him for. But decisions must remain with you. The consultant cannot carry the ultimate responsibility. He *does* have a responsibility to state his views when he disagrees with you. Nonetheless, if he is involved in implementation he must thereafter do his best to implement your decisions.

If you feel you have a genuine grievance with a consultant, *complain.* Preferably to the top. Several consulting companies respond to all client complaints, no matter how small, with a visit from a member of the top management. This not only settles grievances quickly, it also discourages overselling at lower levels and normally improves the quality of service for many months thereafter.

Be wary of charges for 20 percent of a man's time, throughout the term of a long project, unless he is the line manager of the assigned consultants or working one day a week on your premises for some other clear reason. For specialists, you often get more for your money if they are spending full-time on your project for shorter portions of its duration.

Be wary also of the open-ended or phaseless contract. Users sometimes underestimate the magnitude of a project, and the consultant cannot know this until he has begun to work on it. But the way to handle this is by means of regular reviews and checkpoints. These can be spelled out in your list of deliverables. Contracts with limits can be extended if necessary by an exchange of letters, but it is much harder to say: "That's enough boys. Go home now," when your consultant is working on an open-ended contract. Just like the high-powered in-house expert, a well-motivated consultant will happily go on and find a never-ending succession of new problems to solve for you unless he's stopped.

Problem solving is less amenable to the fixed-price contract, but if this is offered by a reputable firm you trust, pay serious attention. If you can assure yourself that the confidence thus expressed is based on a thorough understanding of the problem rather than a foolhardy technological optimism, this kind of "systems contract" tends to put the risk in the hands of the consultancy. Make sure you have measurable output in the form of implementation. In this kind of contract (which is similar to turn-key contracting and discussed in detail in Chapter 9), it is better to have results than advice. It is also wise to have the deliverables include not only the system itself but also reviews and checkpoints. This is not only to reassure yourself but also to maintain communications channels with the consulting firm.

Most consulting contracts are written on a time-and-materials basis, but this need not mean that the time is unlimited. In many cases the on-going relationship can be maintained with payment of a fairly small retainer, which covers regular "servicing" visits. These can be a healthy phenomenon, though they tend to be a trifle sales-oriented. Remember that the consultant has no other sales medium than his personal contact with you. He cannot remind you with clever TV ads that it is time to go into the next phase of the stock control system, or look at documentation for the new process control programs. These visits can be useful because the consultant generally talks to people involved in the operation of previous systems, and can sometimes see problems developing before management is aware of them, or see opportunities to use existing equipment in new ways at minimum expense. If his implementation included training your staff (the best implementations usually do), he will also have a chance to evaluate the level of training and see how your people have maintained and extended the work since his departure.

Measuring the performance of a consultant when he has been working on a highly technical problem seems difficult. However, the results of his efforts should eventually show up on the corporate balance sheet, in improved efficiency, a better level of competence in your own staff, and improved profits (unless you were computerizing the wrong things).

Before you choose a consulting company, you check its references, asking previous clients such questons as:

- the nature of the work done
- the competence of the individual consultants assigned to do it
- how well they worked with the client's staff
- how well they themselves were supervised by their firm
- how effective were the solutions they proposed or implemented
- whether the assignment was completed within the time and cost estimates
- the benefits achieved
- whether the consultants would be hired again

The best way to evaluate the work of the consulting company after your project is finished is simply to ask yourself the same questions.

In checking references, and later among your own people, you will encounter the dual-parentage phenomenon. The consultant has described how he had full responsibility for implementing the personnel information system at Bloggs. Then the Bloggs people tell you how they implemented their personnel information system and were quite pleased, incidentally, with a little help the consultant gave them on the training and installation. You'll hear phrases like: "Ah, yes. They took some of the details off your shoulders so we could get on with the systems design." Don't worry too much about this kind of discrepancy. The consultant is almost always an adviser, so the client indeed had full responsibility. If the training was done tactfully and well, the client will feel the resulting system is really his own doing. Much more important is the satisfaction with the system itself. Watch out for the orphan project where neither the client nor the consultant wishes to take the credit.

THE VIEW FROM THE OTHER SIDE

To a man, consultants stress the importance of client cooperation. "The consulting relationship is a very personal one," says G. E. Williams, a London-based strategic consultant. "For me it works best when I know the chief executive, his policies, and his problems, well enough to act as his extension, an extra set of eyes and ears tuned especially to the flow of information through the company."

Another consultant notes that as with other things in life, you get out of a consulting relationship just about what you put into it. "The client can't just sit back and let the consultant get on with it," he comments. "It is certainly no accident that some of the most satisfied users of consultants are among the largest and most successful companies. They knew what they wanted. They recognized the contribution that a competent consultant could make. And they were prepared to play their part in achieving the desired results."

Dr. Maurice Kendall, chairman of Scicon, adds another observation: start slow. "I favor the ecological approach," he says. "If you want to grow trees in sand, you first sow grass. Then you sow shrubs. Finally you plant trees. Most companies are only in the grass stage now when it comes to using computers and consultants profitably. We have the technology, the analysts, the electronics. But to get a major project off the ground you need *time*—to get used to new systems or databases and find out what you can do with the equipment or information you already have—before you can evaluate the future needs and bigger systems sensibly."

5

Making, Buying, and Selling Software

If the mainframe in a computer system is analogous to the engine in a car, then the software must be the drive shaft, wheels, and controls that make the power useful. Some portions are an integral part of the structure like the differential gear in your car. Others, like the muffler or bumpers, make it pleasant, convenient, or safe to drive. Still others, like statuary on the radiator cap, are sheer furbelows—luxurious if you can afford them, but quite unrelated to the functioning of the system. Software can make the difference between running like a Ford or a Ferrari.

A few brief definitions may cut through the awe and mystique that have grown up to surround software.

MANAGEMENT TRANSLATOR

Instruction: in the software sense, a single line of code related to one or more hardware instructions that force the computer to do something.

Program: a set of instructions that tell the computer how to do a specific job. Programs can be written at different levels:

Machine language: indecipherable nonsense to nonprogrammer humans, but easily decoded by the computer, with a line of code equal to a machine instruction.

Assembly language: in ascending order of complexity, one assembly language instruction can create a few lines of machine code and is vaguely comprehensible to humans.

High-level language: one high-level language instruction can create dozens of machine-language instructions. High-level languages can be created for different specialists outside the computer business, so this instruction may be more meaningful to an accountant than it is to a programmer.

Programs can be broken down into *routines* (which do specific portions of the job) and *subroutines* (still smaller segments, often reusable). Some programs are also organized into *modules* that fit together in different arrangements to make different programs.

Package: is a group of related programs, sometimes able to use the same information. The term is also used to refer to any program that is sold (in a package with its documentation) to anyone who has a suitable computer.

Operating System: is the instructions that control the computer itself. They work with and through the hardware controller to shunt bits around from storage, the arithmetic unit, and the I/O system. The operating system is usually supplied by the computer manufacturer. Generically, it is often referred to as *OS*, but IBM has both OS and DOS (disk operating system) to confuse the issue (not to mention AOS and TOS and various others). Ignore the acronyms assiduously.

Compiler: is both the dictionary and the machinery for a high-level language. It runs through the user's high-level instructions, translating each one into a number of machine-level instructions and fitting them together. Because different compilers for the same language do this fitting together differently (sometimes quick-and-dirty for once-off programs, sometimes passing through quite a few times to squeeze out the last bit of efficiency), it is impossible to compare A's FORTRAN to B's FORTRAN unless you know what kind of jobs it is to do.

Interpreter: works like a compiler, except that it checks its translation of each line with the user before it goes on to the next.

System software: is the traffic policeman that controls the priority and order of things. The term is usually used to refer to the operating system and any other programs such as debugging routines or compilers that are used to make the machine run rather than do a specific task.

Applications software: is the conglomeration of programs that do your job rather than IBMs. Some purists prefer to reserve the term "software" only for the system software, and refer to "applications programs" instead. Other purists (notably software houses) insist that the term software should extend to anything that isn't hardware, such as feasibility studies, training, or documentation. Software houses would like to do more of these kinds of software jobs.

Programmer: is an expensive young man or woman who writes the instructions to the computer. You are not expected to question his attire or the posters on his wall unless you are T. J. Watson, Jr., whose last published act before he retired as chairman of IBM was to reestablish a sense of community at Armonk by reminding the troops that long hair and pink shirts are *not* IBM.

Systems analyst: is an even more expensive person who has enough common sense and communication skill to go out to various departments in the company and translate their jumbled noncomputer tasks into step-by-step, orderly charts, of exactly what must be done and in which order, and why. Like ladies and women, almost all systems analysts have been programmers, but not all programmers are capable of being systems analysts. It can safely be assumed that all programmers (as well as all computer operators and most mailboys) expect to become systems analysts very rapidly. The term is sometimes overused; the man who designs new forms for the mailroom is doing systems analysis of a sort, but it is not usually necessary to pay him at the same level, so it would be wise to reserve the title for the more rare computer variety.

Systems synthesis: is my own term to describe something beyond systems analysis. The best analysts go down to the bare bones of the department's task and come up again to *synthesize* a system including the people and procedures that accomplish the task, perhaps in a fundamentally different way. For example, look at a payroll; 99.9 percent of payroll programs reproduce the procedures that went before. This is the result of lower-level systems analysis. Systems synthesis would say: "These work from personnel records. Therefore, you don't have just a payroll system, you have personnel files and timekeeping." In this context, payroll is a few programs that extract information from personnel files and do simple manipulations with it, perhaps feeding back updated information as necessary.

Software house: is a company with its own consultants, systems analysts, and/or programmers that will happily write programs for you, for a fee. When you need a program, you have to decide whether to do it yourself, bring in people from a software house to do it alongside your people, send the job out to the software house and tell them not to come back until it works, or find someone who has already done just such a program and buy it ready-made. All four paths are littered with little traps.

OPERATING SYSTEMS

When your people are planning to buy a new computer, upgrade an existing one, or even use a bureau, one of their first considerations must be the operating system. Version 18.5 of OS with MFT and QTAM (don't worry about those) may be much nicer than the old DOS system, but it will probably require a much bigger mainframe, some extra peripherals, and rewriting of most of your programs.

It is axiomatic that most of your programmers and systems analysts will prefer the newer, fancier operating system. Before the decision is made, it is probably wise to bring in an expert for an objective review. One bureau was considering switching to a newly announced computer whose operating system was still in a gauche adolescent stage. The consultant commented: "It will run absolutely anything, so long as it's DOS/COBOL."

"That's fine," his client responded. "It saves me £2000 a month, and I don't want them doing anything but DOS/COBOL anyway. If it did all those other things it's promising, I'd be in trouble."

Because the operating systems are furnished by the manufacturer, they come in a range of sizes and styles, like off-the-rack clothes, to more or less fit most users. As a result, there is a tremendous temptation among bright programmers and DP managers to do minor alterations. Some features aren't used at all. Other housekeeping routines fit awkwardly, and make setup or running times longer. It would only take six man-months to tune it up so you could handle 50 simultaneous users instead of 41.

At all costs, resist the temptation. The unhappiest users (and a large percentage of defunct bureaus) are those that tinkered with their operating systems. This is the most complicated part of the entire computer. The few people in the world who really understand the innards of an operating system are receiving huge salaries from the computer manufacturers, and, even so, most operating systems have trouble living up to their specifications. One operating system for time sharing that was described in the present tense in a 1966 brochure finally arrived on the market in rudimentary form in 1971, and version number two was already necessary to add some of the missing features that had been rashly written into a few 1968 contracts.

If you make changes to your operating system, the manufacturer will seldom accept responsibility for the results. You also lock yourself out of later versions, where the changes may be made for you. It is much more practical to send your bright lads to the next few meetings of the manufacturer's user group, backing up their demands for changes with a barrage of politely irate letters of your own to the chairman, the PR director, the head of software, or your aunt who is a stockholder.

Even if you have the rare expert who knows operating systems inside out, you can't beat the system. "Temporarily, yes," says one such treasure. "You can optimize a little. But permanently, no. They will come back with a new operating system. It's not usually worth optimizing a moving target."

Though operating systems are usually unsatisfactory (which leads to such temptation), their future directions are fairly clear. Eventually, they must manage a number of intermediary processors (collections of languages and housekeeping features that might be termed "minioperating systems" themselves) that in turn have subprocessors, each taking care of its own users and range of special languages. In the ideal system, these would all be able to read and write the same file structures (no matter what the language) so they could work from the same information without wiping each other out. This is beginning to happen, but it is unlikely to be common before the 1980s.

The intimate relationship between the operating system and computer hardware is also receiving attention that will bring advances. At Oxford University, Christopher Strachey uses a little computer, primarily working toward a mathematical and theoretical basis for computer languages. As he has been exploring these badly needed fundamentals, he has also been taking data on the behavior of the machine and its operating system.

Using a statistics-gathering interpreter (which slows down the machine too much for normal use in business), Strachey found that less than 2 percent of the operating system accounts for almost the whole of the time—transferring compilers in and out of core. In other words, if the portions that did this task were kept in especially rapid storage, the whole system would run much faster. In one day, Strachey's statistics-gatherer collected information on about 200 million machine-language instructions obeyed, which is a large enough sample to be called real statistics rather than artificial ones. He found that four machine instructions accounted for 50 percent of the total obeyed instructions, and 13 accounted for over 90 percent of the total. A single pair, to store one logical result and load the next, accounted for 20 percent of the total. If these were run together as a single instruction, most users would save about 10 percent of their computer resources.

HIGH-LEVEL LANGUAGES

The quickest way to start an argument among a group of computer professionals is to say: "Why don't we standardize on APL?" (or Cobol, or any other language). Proponents and opponents to any language materialize magically, already waving their arms and prepared to do battle unto death for their favorite.

This is not as strange as it seems—the languages are the personality of the computer. Each computer has a different compiler for each language (sometimes several—there are debug compilers, optimizing compilers, student-crunching compilers, conversational compilers, and more). Most computers have at least several general-purpose languages (these include BASIC, FORTRAN, COBOL, PL/1, ALGOL, and APL). Each compiler for each language was written by a few human beings (the fewer the better), who in the process expressed their own views of how computers ought to work, what users wanted, and how they related to their machines. The droll little FORTRAN compiler for the old SDS 9300 computer was written by two droll little men who included such pleasantries as "Your missing END statement has been supplied by courtesy of SDS." People who liked their computers to be personable were delighted. A few "let's get on with it" sorts would have preferred "Missing END statement."

Like operating systems, high-level languages came into use in the early sixties as computer usage outgrew the ability of machine-language programmers to keep up with the demand for programs. Formerly they had to reinvent the series of instructions every time for even the simplest sequence of events. "Add X to Y" was an incomprehensible series of instructions, and if 25 programmers were asked to write a routine, 25 different routines invariably resulted. In high-level language you would still get 25 different routines, but the "Add X to Y" sequence can be expressed in terms similar to "$X + Y = ?$" (its exact form depending on the language). The language is where the human being actually communicates with the computer (and vice versa), so the development of high-level languages made it possible for more people to write their own programs.

It is not necessary to understand the nuances and differences among languages in order to have a successful computer installation in your company. A quick summary should suffice to squelch arguments.

COBOL: is the most frequently used language in business. It stands for COmmon Business-Oriented Language. Univac and the U.S. Navy, spearheaded by an iron-willed wispy lady in her sixties named Grace Hopper, have done a great deal to standardize COBOL among the different manufacturers, with the result that the first standard data management systems (see Chapter 6) are likely to be created for COBOL users.

RPG: (Report Program Generator) is not exactly a high-level language, but is used by many smaller IBM installations, which means a large proportion of the user population. It is a stripped-down language, strictly for business, that can spit out reports in ordinary business formats and set up the programs necessary for ordinary business calculations.

FORTRAN: (FORmula TRANslator) is the most popular language for scientific calculations, and has been extended to business fairly successfully, particularly through time-sharing systems. There are also versions such as SUPER-FORTRAN, XTRAN (which must stand for EXTRA-SUPER-FORTRAN), and so on.

PL/1: (Programming Language/1) is IBM's candidate for a computer lingua franca. Thus it has the best chance of achieving that desired goal. Academics tend not to like it, commenting that it is an elephant, invented by a committee (one that contained few academics). Certainly in its early days, PL/1's ambitious attempts to be all things to all users simply led to a proliferation of committees, versions, and confusion. The latest versions have been moderately successful, and many companies that still use FORTRAN and COBOL for updating their earlier programs are turning to PL/1 for new programs. Most business programmers like it, though it still has too many features, nuances, options, frills, and furbelows that are used only by a handful, and clutter up the language and the documentation for the rest. I would not dispute IBM's contention that when (or if) standardization finally comes, you'll find 20 percent of scientific programs written in FORTRAN, 20 percent of business programs written in COBOL, and most of the remaining 60 percent in PL/1, though it is likely to be PL/2 or so by that time.

ALGOL: (ALGOrithmic Language) is an elegant thing, beloved in its latest versions by academics, particularly in Europe, where more work has been done on specifying and standardizing it. It runs superbly on Burroughs' latest computers, which were designed by ALGOL people. Because IBM does not share Burroughs' enthusiasm, ALGOL is likely to achieve the status of escargots, the spicy hors d'oeuvres for cognoscenti, while PL/1 takes the hamburger and roast beef market. An *algorithm*, incidentally, is a mathematical procedure or pattern for solving some particular class of problems.

BASIC: (Business And Scientific Interactive Compiler) was developed at Dartmouth College for one of the first time-sharing systems. It has become a standard language for time sharing (followed closely by FORTRAN), and has spawned as many versions and superversions as there are time-sharing computers, plus a few extra from superbureaus. BASIC is particularly easy to learn; in some versions it can be used successfully within several hours.

APL: (A Programming Language) was developed at IBM, but came into more general use, especially in commercial time-sharing systems, very much against IBM's passive resistance. (IBM characteristically maintains a number of parallel research activities in hardware or software, then cuts off the majority, even though they may indeed be quite workable, when it has decided which way the trade winds are blowing and which breezes are most likely to lead to long-term profit. The other manufacturers would like to be able to do the same, but can't afford as much research.) In the case of APL, passionate support from a few users eventually led to some measure of support for the language. Originally designed for algebra classes, it uses a number of algebra symbols, but the language is very pleasant to work with from an IBM typewriter terminal, and the latest versions have some data management features that make it very nice for business. It still requires the programmer to think about his payroll problem as if it were a matrix, and the time card as a vector, which limits its usefulness. Nonetheless, it is very concise, and will probably achieve standardization, particularly for design programmers who are building large systems.

RATIONALIZING BABELGOL[1]

No installation can afford the specialists it would take to keep up with developments in all these languages. No computer manufacturer (with one exception) can afford the specialists it would take to create all the compilers needed to support each of the general high-level languages. Even

1. The word *Babelgol* is attributed to Norwegian consultant Norman Sanders.

IBM would rather concentrate its efforts in applications and operating systems, once the language-proliferation problem can be solved.

There are two forms of standardization in the computer industry: through decisions made by official committees of users and manufacturers, and through decisions made by IBM. In many cases, the latter is the quickest solution. However, because languages are the emotional tie between users and computers, not even IBM can dictate standards overnight. FORTRAN was IBM's own development, but a business language called COMTRAN ran into COBOL head-on. After a year or so, COMTRAN gave way gracefully, and IBM came out with its own COBOL.

If you are changing from one machine to another, or using a bureau machine that differs from your own, beware of the supersubset. Specifications have been developed for standardizing some languages, but these are tremendously complex, and the new language must include all the nuances of your old one to be able to run your present programs properly. There's FORTRAN II, FORTRAN IV, FORTRAN IV Level H, SUPER-FORTRAN, and COBOL F *or* ANSI COBOL. When IBM decided to wipe out COBOL F and replace it with ANSI (American National Standards Institute) COBOL, users in the United States alone spent between $2,000,000,000 and $3,000,000,000 to convert their programs.

Just as different operating systems exact different "overhead" costs for some types of jobs, languages differ widely in their efficiency. The ADD instruction in COBOL can do its job with anything from three to thirty assembly-level instructions (with a further magnification at the machine's own level) depending on the compiler and the manufacturer.

No universal high-level language is ever likely, or desirable for that matter. PL/1's attempt to be all things to all men has already taken more than seven years to reach a sensible implementation, and FORTRAN and COBOL show no signs of dying out as a result. All three have been submitted to American and European groups for standardization; the various levels are now accepted as having certain well-specified characteristics. The greatest arguments are continuing to rage over whether these specified floors should also be ceilings. Most users would probably be better off if they were; if every ANSI COBOL were exactly like every other ANSI COBOL, with no added options or features, this would make programmers as well as programs more transferable. The strongest voices in the floor-equals-ceiling argument are knowledgeable users.

One major problem with standardization is the time it takes, in human terms. IBM can afford to send a man to meetings of the volunteer Codasyl group trying to standardize data management, month after month, year after year. The man can (and did) submit 71 amendments, then vote against the final recommendation (which passed anyway). IBM can then decide whether or not to go along with the recommendation; if it does, it will probably do so with reluctance. For companies that are not primarily in the computer business but must depend on the computers in other parts of their work, this kind of investment of capable people is a burden, and must inevitably be chalked up as a public service rather than an investment that will bring returns in the foreseeable future. Those companies that have carried this burden on behalf of other users for the past few years deserve some appreciation from other computer users, who are beginning to benefit from the growing power of the standardization groups. If you are lucky enough to hire one of the rare men who are so capable in languages that they are invited to participate in one of these time-consuming but exhilarating groups, encouraging him will not only earn his loyalty, but also raise morale (and up-to-date knowledge) in the rest of your computer department.

A good general-purpose language has been defined as one in which you can build good special-purpose languages. These are such things as FFL (First Financial Language), Square (which has an on-line PL/1), Xtat (a statistical language for the 360/67) or Fore (an on-line report generator). They can be purchased from computer manufacturers, from universities, or from users who have developed them to do specific tasks. You can develop your own special-purpose language if you need it badly enough and no outside language is available. If all your Widget engineers are working on the in-house system through terminals, and finding too many limitations in FORTRAN when it comes to widgetry, the investment may be worthwhile—if you have a first-class language man or two. If you don't, don't bother trying to develop them, though there will be plenty of volunteers.

APPLICATIONS PROGRAMMING

Special-purpose languages (and general-purpose languages) are the basic materials from which applications programs are written—the programs that work for your company directly, processing its particular tasks through the computer. The room full of programmers and systems analysts exists in your company simply to write applications programs or bring old ones up to date.

Far more than in choosing operating systems or languages, this is where the user can control his costs. Managing the programmers is not just a matter of seeing that they write the requisite number of instructions every week and turn out bug-free programs that do the job, but also of choosing which jobs to do. Many installations carry out a feasibility study when they start out to computerize a task, but very few do a comparable study when programs must be upgraded.

For companies with centralized computer operations, it is usually sensible to work like a service bureau or software house, with the central department charging user departments for its services. They will get into the same sorts of squabbles. The traditional argument runs something like: "You have changed the specs, so we had to charge you more" versus "You programmed it too slowly, so we had to change our specs."

A formal procedure for developing new applications programs and a stripped-down version for upgrading old ones can avoid endless squabbles and save money. The diagram in Figure 5-1 looks complicated, but by rigorously following these steps, Hill, Samuel & Company, Ltd., has been able to do major banking applications as well as minor programs with considerable success. The job is normally broken down into stages and each begins with a formal assignment, accompanied by specific management directives. It finishes with a formal presentation of a report by the computer department's project team (including one or two full-time representatives from the user department) before the user department issues the directive to start the next stage. Stages 4 and 5 can be telescoped when a single program rather than a number of them is being considered for an entire application (for example, stock control).

One key document in this procedure is the feasibility study report. This contains a summary of the conclusions; backed up by descriptions of the alternative solutions that were considered; an outline of the solution that is recommended (and why); the expected benefits in financial, manpower, control, and information availability terms; the organizational effects; an implementation schedule; and cost estimates. Simply having to produce this information in written form acts as a control on enthusiasms of the computer department, and gives a useful reference for postmortems if things go wrong or for historical comparison if an application is being enhanced or upgraded.

In a large company, particularly one where computing has gone through a decentralization phase, it is entirely too common to find that three departments are all developing programs with identical routines, or identical goals but different names (and completely different ways of ac-

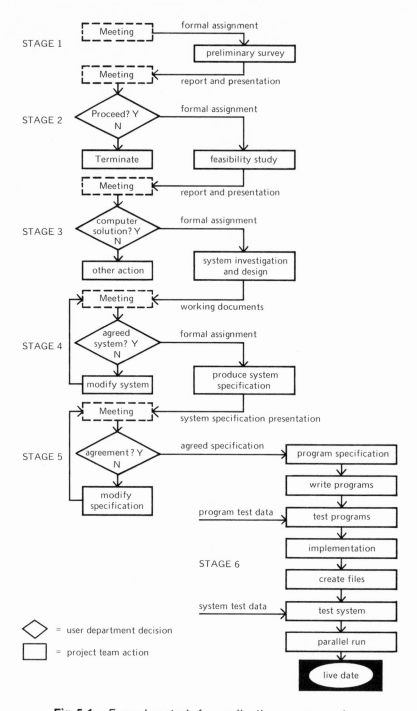

Fig. 5-1. Formal controls for applications programming.

74

complishing their tasks). One way to keep this expensive duplication to a minimum is to make sure the feasibility studies for computer applications are reviewed at one central point, even with a decentralized installation. Another control is to create an internal software "directory," listing all the programs in use within the various departments (with simple translations of their functions if possible), as well as the programs currently under development. If this is simple and easy to use, and if programs are easily transferable from one department to another (both technically and administratively), less wheels are likely to be reinvented.

PACKAGES—HOW TO BUY THEM

Somewhere back in the Stone Age someone invented the wheel. Cart makers, toy makers, and car makers have been trying to improve on it ever since. If your programming people insist that they must have a program to handle names and addresses, it is reasonable to assume that other companies have had the same need. A wheel for your name and address system may already be available at a reasonable cost.

There are three major problems with packaged programs: finding them, evaluating them, and supporting them. The amount of time (and money) spent in each of these activities should bear some reasonable relationship to the cost of doing it yourself and the value of the program to your own company. A rudimentary feasibility study can establish these levels.

Packaged programs come from many sources. Your computer manufacturer has already bombarded your computer people with literature about all his program products that might be suitable for your installation. Others have been developed by bureaus or software houses, either as entrepreneurial ventures or sponsored by users who needed them. A number of highly successful user-developed programs are available in packaged form, though these are sometimes harder to find and are not always as well documented or supported as their brethren from computer industry companies. Trade associations and industry conventions can sometimes reveal these, or lead to meetings with other users who have similar needs.

There are several publications that can take some of the pain out of package hunting. The *ICP Quarterly*[2] lists about 2000 programs from over

2. *ICP Quarterly* is published by International Computer Programs, Inc., at 2511 East 46th Street, Indianapolis, Indiana 46205. It costs $100 per year.

500 companies; no attempt is made to evaluate the programs beyond the demand that they be documented, but they are indexed by industry (everything from "accounting, small business" to "utilities industry"), by hardware configuration (over 350 are listed for the 360/30 alone), and alphabetically by name. The indexes make the book a fairly useful clearinghouse.

Auerbach Publishers Inc.[3] has sifted through more than 9000 packaged programs to produce evaluations of about 3000. The level of support and sophistication required by potential customers differs widely, of course, but an Auerbach listing, like a Dun & Bradstreet listing, can eliminate unnecessary headaches and give an indication of whether a program matches your ability to support or amend it. Other groups such as the National Computing Centre or Co-Pac Index in Britain and *Datamation* magazine in America, as well as trade associations, also maintain lists of packages, some of them written up with user comments.[4]

Whatever the source, it makes sense to ask for references, and to check them carefully, preferably by seeing the package in operation. If this is not possible, don't buy before you have had a trial run on your own machine, with your own data.

Packages can be sold, leased, licensed, borrowed, or rented. The selling (or leasing, licensing, borrowing, or renting) charge for a package seldom bears much relationship to the cost of developing the package. It is much more an expression of what the originator thinks the market will bear. Thus there are some very good bargains to be had in packages. There are also some overpriced monstrosities. There is also considerable room for bargaining, particularly if you are going to be amending an industry-oriented package from another user.

Various companies take different approaches to protect their packages from pilferage; copying a magnetic tape is entirely too easy, and thefts have been common. No method is completely effective. Several bureaus, preferring not to share royalties, have copied one leading forecasting package. The expense and time of a lawsuit are seldom worth the trouble.

One of the best methods of protection also ensures that the user makes

3. Auerbach Publishers Inc. is located at 121 North Broad Street, Philadelphia, Pennsylvania 19107.

4. A useful paper on buying packages was presented by John Mills, regional manager of Britain's National Data Processing Service, at the May 1971 seminar of the International Federation of Information Processing Societies, in Stockholm. An article based on the paper is available in the May 1971 issue of *Computer Management* (196 Shaftesbury Avenue, London WC2).

his monthly payments on time. The package is sent out as a deck of cards with a built-in self-destruct instruction on a specified date. If the payment does not arrive on time, the new deck is not sent out.

Besides the credentials of the originator and references from other users, check very carefully for extra costs and for such important support factors as fitting it into your version of the operating system. You may be expected to pay the travel and expenses of the vendor's people while they install the package.

Applications programs (by far the largest class of packages) traditionally require more modification than systems packages or programmer aids. This makes sense. The programs that have been written by programmers for programmers, such as automatic flow-charting packages, are usually more successful than programs written by programmers for accountants or engineers (unless there was a real accountant or engineer on the implementation team). Even an awkward, ill-fitting application program may be worth fixing up in comparison with the cost of writing it from scratch.

Overengineering a program is expensive, whether you do it to your own program or someone else's. There is often a delicate trade-off between the cost of amendments and the cost of changing the (human) procedures within your company to fit the demands of the generalized package. The cost of disgruntled employees and errors during the learning period for the new procedures should be added into the estimates when you are making package make-or-buy decisions.

Documentation can take any form, or no form. So make sure you see it before you buy. If you are purchasing the package, you will probably have to promise to use it only for your own company, or even for one installation within your own company, but you can ask for sufficient documentation to maintain or amend the package yourself. The most professionally packaged products come with easily understood instructions for operators and terminal users as well as programmers.

The level of support will probably affect the monthly charge for the package, though some of the best sellers can spread their expenses across a larger number of customers and give first-class support. This is particularly true when the package is one of the vendor's primary sources of revenue. If you are buying from a user, make sure the contract spells out very clearly how much help you can expect on installation, then maintenance, and then divide by two for the latter, particularly if the package is purchased rather than rented. (Multiply by two the in-house estimates of support costs.) Contractual squabbles with vendors can sometimes be arbitrated by such professional groups as the Association for Computing Machinery or the British Computer Society, with or without recourse to law.

Many standard packaged programs are also available from bureaus. Here most of the support problems belong to somebody else. It is in the bureau's best interest to train your people to use the package because charges are usually made on a use-plus-royalty basis. If you are interested in a package for in-house use, ask the vendor if it is available on a bureau. If so, you can try it out painlessly and invest for your own system only if your level of use will save money over the bureau charges.

PACKAGES—HOW TO SELL THEM

Your people have just come back from the Widget convention reporting that the application they finished last month for Widget inventory control is clearly ahead of anything else on the market. They have been approached by five other widget makers who would like to buy the package if they can get it for less than $100,000. You have three choices.

You can keep it as a secret weapon, keeping your stock levels more cost-effective than anyone else's. If you do, your competitors will undoubtedly develop their own applications, possibly hiring away your best programmers to do so. The most you gain is a little time.

You can casually sell it "as is" for $99,000 to the five competitors, perhaps sweetening the pot with a couple of days for one of your boys to go over and tell them how it works. If it doesn't, they may sue you or something similarly unpleasant, so it is best to make sure that the documentation is already sufficient for your own noncomputer people, that some training notes are available, and that the specification is clear enough for another company to understand. It may also need "denaturing." There's no sense telling them *too* much about the equations you use to determine your own inventory levels. A few more sales might result by hearsay.

Your third choice is to go into the package-selling business. If you think the market is large enough, and if you think you are more likely than some software outfit to know where that market is and how to sell to it, the diversification may be worthwhile. It will also require the same administrative support that any new product takes: a marketing team; distribution and installation people; further research and product improvement; professional documentation training, program maintenance, and modification. You are in the software business overnight.

For most companies, the middle road is probably the most practical. If the application is a fairly large one and specific to your own industry, you can charge a higher fee for it than you could if you generalized it for a larger market (in itself a major task). With outright sale to a few well-known companies in your own industry, you have less worry about theft—they have no reason to pass the expensive creature on to yet other competitors—though someone else may choose to undertake the generalizing and selling. Any salable program that is so sufficiently documented and/or supported that it can be used by a potential buyer can be listed in the *ICP Quarterly* for a small fee.

If your program obviously has a wider market, but you don't want to sell it yourself, you can make arrangements with a reputable software company to handle the marketing—and preferably the support as well.

This may be your best test of its marketability. If leading software houses refuse to handle it, you might be foolhardy to continue trying. John Hoskyns, chairman of one of Britain's largest software houses, has commented: "One of the things that makes top management very ready to listen to their DP people talk about diversifying into services is the fact that they know they have made a major investment (if investment is the right word) in developing their own software in the past. It is very attractive to want to believe that you can recoup this investment. But what you are really doing (obviously there will be exceptions that prove the rule) is deluding yourself in some cases into believing that the mass of bloodstained software which you now have in the basement in bits and pieces, badly documented, never very satisfactory, and most of it obsolete, developed over the last five or ten years, is in fact a thoroughly market-researched, superbly engineered product ready to go straight to a carefully selected market."

Some kinds of programs (for example, Hill Samuel's share registration suite) lend themselves to distribution on a service basis rather than packaging. Hill Samuel's share registration group evolved into a separate corporate entity as demand for the service grew. This can be sensible. Chapter 11 deals with some of the perils of the in-house/out-house bureau.

In some cases, a few companies in an industry band together to retain a software company to write a major application that would otherwise be too expensive for any one of them. (As in any other software assignment, the credentials of the company should be scrutinized carefully.) If the software company wants to sell the resulting application (preferably returning royalties to the sponsors), make sure the chosen vendor is prepared to support it properly; your name is inevitably associated with the product. It is also wise to specify how many interruptions your people are willing to put up with to show the package in operation to prospective buyers.

CHOOSING AND USING A SOFTWARE HOUSE

Having a program written for you by a software house involves a new professional relationship, just like that with the consultant. In fact, some of the most reputable software houses are also first-class computer consultancies. Others, equally reputable, are small groups of specialists in particular kinds of software: compilers, business programs, telecommunications. Still others are "body shops," hiring out programmers of a certain certified level for short- or medium-term assignments. You can order a PL/1 programmer with inventory control experience for three months, or a COBOL payroll man who knows the Univac 1108 for three weeks. One programmer was simply given a wodge of specifications and told: "Write as much JCL (job control language) as possible in three weeks." He did, with respectable results as it turned out, but this is not usually the best way to use people from a software house.

If you are putting your application in the hands of a software house, you deserve some reassurance that it will continue to exist long enough to provide you with a finished, workable program. Check on its turnover, how long it has been in business, its current financial situation (if possible), the qualifications of its staff members, and how suited they are in languages and applications for your particular job. Software houses have gone through a period of rapid growth with severe ups and downs, partly because they tend to attract some of the brightest programmers (who are often volatile and youthful sorts), partly because it is very easy to start a software house and carry it through its early stages without much business experience or financial backing. A company that has been in business for a few years has probably mastered some of the necessary techniques for project control, too.

For best results, the original planning should be carried out in-house, possibly with someone from the software house sitting in. Whether the software house takes over at that stage and conducts the actual feasibility study, or whether you wait until after the feasibility study to hand over the task, it would be wise to follow the same rigorous procedure of meetings and checkpoints, with written assignments and reports, that works for in-house projects. Company involvement is even more important because outside programmers are not familiar with your own corporate procedures and quirks, and may make assumptions based on general practice that do not fit your particular situation. The sooner these are caught, the less they are likely to cost. If the software house specializes in the particular application you want, a high level of interaction may allow it to suggest more efficient or less expensive ways of getting the job done if you involve its people at the earliest stages.

A clear specification, no matter who developed it, should be agreed upon between your company and the software house. This will smooth the process considerably. So will a clear contract, setting out which party is responsible for what inputs and when. If your people do not furnish sample data for program tests on time, the software house cannot be blamed for the delay. ACM or BCS and most of the larger software houses can show sample contracts that cover most contingencies. If they have worked all the way through on the assumption that you must be using version 18.5 of the operating system, while you have had to settle for version 14 because some bright changes were made in-house a couple of years ago, there will be an enormous squabble at the end when the program doesn't work on your system.

Software houses are beginning to take on larger "systems contracts," in which they provide not only the programs but often the equipment, packages, training, and special devices (for example, banking terminals) to make it work. A few are very well qualified for this kind of work. Others are not, but know not that they are not. Rather than being the unfortunate who brings about this revelation, it would be sensible to check references, preferably for jobs of similar size, or for similar applications. The ability to move up from simple coding to fancier programming and applications specialties is a mark of maturity in the software industry, but project management for major systems is a skill that can be very expensive to learn. This does not mean that large systems should *not* be farmed out. A systems contract with a reputable software house, working closely with your people, may be the best way to achieve a major system that has quite a bit of pioneering content. The systems contract (which differs from a turnkey contract in the amount of user involvement along the way) should mean the software house is willing to stand behind the resulting system on the basis of its performance. Ways of measuring or evaluating this should therefore be specified.

GETTING MORE FOR YOUR SOFTWARE MONEY

All the developments that make programs easier to write and more likely to work are going to cost extra computer time to run and need more space to store. The most promising techniques—modular programming and high-level languages—seem to justify the expense. Because hardware costs are falling even faster than programmer salaries are rising, the investment in extra storage is already justified in most cases, and looks better every year.

Debugging programs (taking out all their little errors) can cost a fortune. It is sometimes better to live with the existing programs, even though they may be slow, than go through the insecticidal expenditures for upgrading them. Program bugs can be like cold germs: you can learn to live with them when they've been around a while. Make sure there is a written record of the nostrums your computer doctors use to cope with their resident bugs. A new operator won't know he always has to push the start button three times to get his program to run properly unless someone has recorded this vital information.

The techniques for getting a higher payoff from your software and your software people can be summarized in a few rules of thumb:

1. Ignore incomprehensible acronyms and insist on explanations in plain English. People who know what they are doing won't find this difficult.
2. Treat the operating system with the respect it deserves. Require the signed approval of the chairman, God, and T. J. Watson, Jr., before you permit any changes in it.
3. Insist on a documented feasibility study for every new program or application. A "justification study" is not the same as a feasibility study.
4. Cost in the human and procedural changes when you are evaluating potential applications.
5. No matter who is doing your software, make sure there are regular meetings, with the user department in charge.
6. Begin new stages of a project only after all parties have agreed to written plans or specifications from the previous stages.

7. Insist that all programs be documented so that you could understand the summaries yourself.
8. Find a good contracts man and involve him in computer activities so he can learn enough to keep you out of trouble with software houses, package vendors, and the computer manufacturer.
9. Know the difference between necessities and luxuries. Don't let the chairman's chauffeur drive around all day just to prove the Rolls Royce is necessary.

6

Using and Misusing Information

Data is the basic fuel for your computing vehicle. Information is its destination. Some of the most severe problems in computing come about because the two are confused. People spend fortunes tuning up their machines to consume more data, faster, just to get to the next gas station and fill up with more data before somebody else does.

Most companies in the British Institute of Management study said they had installed their first computer systems to improve management information. Yet an Institute of Personnel Management survey[1] of 16 large companies that have computerized their personnel information systems revealed that less than half had tried to analyze the costs versus the benefits, and even less knew what the system was costing them at all. The two that did have this information said the system was costing £3.50 to £4.00 per year per employee. This amounts to at least £40,000 (equivalent to about $100,000) even for the smallest companies in the survey, which had about 10,000 employees. Some companies had average answers to ad hoc personnel inquiries in as little as two hours, while at least one was tolerating response times that *averaged* two months. The norm for all the companies was two weeks.

A classic McKinsey report[2] states: "The most ingenious new proposal may be merely a fancy new wrapping for an outmoded product. Instant

1. *Personnel Records and the Computer: A Survey,* Joan Springall, Institute of Personnel Management and The Industrial Society, London, 1970, £3.

2. *Unlocking the Computer's Profit Potential,* McKinsey & Company, London or New York, 1968, available at no charge.

access to data generated by an outmoded cost accounting system, for example, is at least a dubious blessing."

Data is simply the bits that stream in and out of computers, or the millions of cards that are piling up in the New York insurance company's 60-story headquarters. The two-foot pile of old newspapers in the garage is data. If you have learned anything useful from them, that is information. All the schedules and lists for the tax man are data. How much you have to pay is information. You can *do* something with it. It helps you or your business achieve goals in some way.

Information theory cuts across the entire spectrum from data to information. It is a mathematically oriented, scientific speciality, but its basic precept (long known to journalists) can be summed up in three words: "man bites dog." The information content is directly related to its surprise value. If dog bites mailman, it's no surprise. If mailman bites dog, the result is eye-catching, and probably goes on the front page for a change of pace.

Thus in business some of the most successful computer systems are based on *exception reporting,* spewing out only the surprises. Normal ranges for orders, inventory levels, salaries, billings, or deliveries are stored in the machine. The only printouts concern the values that go outside the expected ranges. These exceptions can then be studied in detail.

GARBAGE-IN/GARBAGE-OUT

Sensible computer people used to have an acronym, GIGO, that stood for "garbage-in/garbage-out." Far too often they were asked to put mountains of data through their machines, creating volumes of reports that were essentially meaningless. Perhaps these were more orderly data, but they seldom contained much information. If there *were* nuggets of information among the garbage, they weren't easy to find.

In recent years, GIGO has developed an alarming permutation: garbage-in/*gospel*-out! The almighty computer, blessing the data with his perfect calculations, is assumed to have created something approaching the status of divine revelation when he prints out a report.

The computer people know better. They realize that the computer is no better than the man who wrote the program, the man who did the systems analysis, and the man who told them what he wanted reported in the first place. The user, who has created this gospel in his own image, then turns against computers when his reports are used to back up decisions that turn out to be wrong, or when they are so late or incomprehensible that they can't be used at all for decision making. He becomes an atheist. The reverse twist is also true too often. Badly designed data can result in a bad reputation for the computer, which inhibits its use in practical applications.

Once it has been completely checked out, a computer is constitutionally unable to make mistakes. Only humans can do that. There are a good many humans in the chain between a request for information and a two-inch stack of printout. The computer can spend hours working out the answers to wrong questions, to twelve-place accuracy. It cannot question simplifying assumptions or procedural decisions that may be wildly wrong. It simply goes on masticating and storing the data dutifully until it is told to spit some out. Whether this is information—management information— is often very questionable indeed.

When Robert McNamara left Ford, where he had been leader of a "whiz kid" management team, to become the U.S. Secretary of Defense, he began to ask questions in the Pentagon. "Why do we need this?" "What will it cost?" "What other ways do we have to achieve this objective?" "What is the cost of not achieving this objective at all?" Consternation was the natural reaction as these questions were amplified and passed down through the ranks, then into the defense and aerospace industries for more and more detailed answers. No one had ever asked such questions before. Soon other people in the chain began asking questions of their own. Eventually the questions led to some very complex and sophisticated systems for feeding back the answers—and controlling projects so that the answers would be satisfactory. Some of these systems were computerized. But the computers never asked the questions. Nor did they answer them. They simply organized and sifted through the masses of data, under the direction of humans, to generate the information that went into the answers.

In theory, company hierarchies exist to carry out the same "systems approach," with a board of directors at the top asking the strategic questions, which the chief executive must ultimately answer. He, in turn, delegates the detailed information-gathering and implementation of overall policies to men at lower levels, and so on down the chain. The more people there are in the chain, the more chances there are that communications will be obstructed and the wrong questions will be answered. Tactical decisions at low levels can alter corporate strategies, and before you know it, someone suggests a computerized management information system to sort things out.

THE MIS MYTH

Management Information Systems (capitalized, as in "A Good Thing" and abbreviated as in MIStake) have been oversold for a decade. Like housewives queuing up to buy laborsaving electric carving knives, managers have responded to the idea of a terminal that would spit out instant answers to all questions at the touch of a button. With few exceptions, the MIS systems that have been computerized are about as laborsaving as electric carving knives, and equally aesthetic, though they cost considerably more.

A classic MIS horror story comes from the U.S. Post Office, which started in 1966 to develop a management information system that would save a projected $4.5 million per year in labor and paperwork, as well as give more timely and accurate reports. In 1971, the U.S. General Accounting Office (GAO) reported that the system was over two years late. Before it is finished, it will cost more than $60 million, although $22.7 million was the sum originally budgeted for the entire job. It has run the post office's costs up, not down, and requires more, not less, people. It has a ferocious error rate. Worst of all, it produces useless reports. GAO blamed the fiasco on inadequate planning, insufficient testing, and too much hurrying at the specification stage.

Several almost-successful systems have been created to give instant answers to relatively unstructured management questions. These have cost tens of millions of dollars, and are still under constant development.

Getting the information requests into a form suitable for a computer has been the problem historically. You can get the entire file out fairly easily. It is the selected portions from different files that cause troubles. Some of the glamour tends to evaporate from MIS if you have to know ahead of time exactly what questions you are going to be asking, then wait several years for development and debugging of a rigid system before you can ask even those.

The computer used to take center stage in a computer system. More and more this focus is shifting to the *file*. The computer is coming to be viewed simply as a machine that handles files with more or less success.

A file inside the computer is not very different from the file in your desk drawer. It holds information. It also holds data. In your drawer file you probably have folders for only the most pressing matters that concern you. Others are stored away in a larger file farther away. Your desk folder may hold everything that concerns this week's crisis, or only the latest information. A secretary once brought order out of her busy executive's chaos by "filing by crisis." Disliking the dreary task, she simply extracted everything that had to do with current and prospective crises, then bundled the rest of the paperwork into a box labeled "to file—September." If a new crisis blew up, she went back over the boxes and extracted the pertinent papers. Her boss never knew the difference—until she departed. Since computers are not creative enough to dislike filing or devise alternatives, they must rely on the inflexible rules laid down by systems analysts— few of whom have spent apprentice time as secretaries or file clerks.

Office files can be stored according to crisis, date, alphabetical order, by subject or person, in chronological order, or in any other system the person in charge of filing has devised. They are thus dependent on the special knowledge or instinct of the file clerk for retrieval.

The computer has no such instinct, and no special knowledge beyond what is bestowed by its human beings in the form of programs. It must have very explicit instructions in order to relate one file to another. Furthermore, the computer file cannot be simply a flexible folder into which papers are inserted. If each file in computer storage had space left for all the possible insertions and changes that might come later, you would quickly run out of storage space (and money). But having too little room is equally difficult because the files become useless if they cannot be kept up to date.

In most systems, a computer file is analogous to a single card in a card file, rather than a folder in a drawer. It has certain identifying information that describes its primary place in the system—like the name and employee number on a personnel card. It has other "fields" for such information as years of service, promotions, salary, attendance record, and so on. In most cases, these are located at exactly the same place within the computer record, just as they are on a printed card, so they can be found quickly and easily. Other systems can accept the information in several formats, so long as the specific fields are preceded by their own identification codes.

The problem comes when you want to relate these fields of information in different ways. For a personnel record alone, the questions might range from: "How long has it been since Jones had an increase in salary?" to "If the labor rates for senior engineers go up by 14 percent, how much will it cost us and who will be affected?" or "Give me a list of all the unmarried draftsmen under 32 who speak German and would not object to a foreign assignment." A personnel clerk with a moderately sized employee file and a few cross-files may be able to handle such information requests. A computer cannot do so without extensive system design and a special program that describes each new desired search through its files.

Multiply the personnel system and the number of kinds of questions you can ask it by the numbers of records you keep for production, marketing, inventory control, distribution, and finance. Then you have some idea of the problems that face MIS designers.

I tend to blame computer manufacturers fairly harshly for the lack of credibility their machines have in business. The skill of the computer architects is often matched only by the temerity of some of the marketing promises. But MIS is one mistake in which the users must share the blame. Customers aren't asking the right questions, even now, and top management seldom asked *any* in the past decade, except: "How soon can we have it?"

The computer salesmen went out, in the mid-sixties, with characteristic promises of marvellous MIS jam tomorrow. In scientific applications this had worked pretty well because the technical men back at the manufactury were able to make good on most of the promises, though performance was always a trifle later than delivery. These MIS promises must have fallen on parched ground because the men began coming back with more and more orders (from customers who should have known better) for systems that simply could not be built. Hardware for such systems was still primitive and expensive—a CRT terminal for less than $5000 was unknown in the mid-sixties. The problems of *storing* large masses of data, much less shifting them around, were almost insurmountable. When the final bids went out with hardware estimates several times as high as the initial promises, and completely open-ended software estimates, there were still companies that insisted on writing blank checks to the computer makers to get MIS. Some of them chose to buy the systems but let their own systems analysts and programmers do the software. These are the battle-scarred men in the user community who now say: "MIS is terribly messy. We still don't know how to do it properly."

DATABASES AND DATABANKS

You don't need a management information system to change your computer philosophy from: "passing data through programs" to the more useful: "passing programs through data." Even program documentation can become data oriented. This is undoubtedly a superior method for systems analysis and programming anyway, but because it differs from traditional ways of thinking in the computer industry, it has not yet come into full bloom. Ten years ago (long before random access or databanks became practical or fashionable), one element of the U.S. government shifted its systems definition and documentation activity to a data-oriented approach instead of a program-oriented one. They quickly found that this was saving them 70 percent or more of their former systems analysis and programming costs. However, even today this is the exception, not the rule. Until this sort of thinking is more prevalent, too many organizations will be in trouble with their databank plans.

Organizing the mountains of data is the first problem. Should it have a treelike hierarchy, with certain types of classification having precedence over others? This means that to relate one twig to another just inches away, you may have to go all the way back to the main trunk and follow another system of branches. If you try to relate every kind of classification to every other, you use up mountains of storage simply filing the necessary cross-lists, until they themselves get hard to find. You could file everything as it arrives, keeping track of the locations and producing up-to-date maps every other minute. The number of possibilities for even a moderate-sized system is enormous. Whatever the technique you choose, the end result is expected to be a database of raw, but retrievable, data, the foundation from which you build an information system.

The term *database* implies a collection of data with a single focus: a personnel database, a credit database, an engineering database. (Some purists prefer to use the term only for elaborate computerized hierarchies, but it is more helpful if you view your pocket list of telephone numbers as a database—a *good* one if it helps you work more effectively.) Companies that specialize in providing information from one database or a number of them are said to maintain "databanks." The word carries financial overtones that imply not only that the various databases have commercial value, but also that they are protected in a manner similar to money in the bank (though this is not always the case).

One of the more promising approaches to database handling is to have a special high-level computer language that frees the user from worrying about the actual physical location of the data, but lets him spell out the various relationships he wants between different kinds of data, fields, or records within his computer files. A few organizations have developed this kind of language for themselves, but it is a very complicated and expensive project. The use of databases is growing very rapidly. Therefore, it will become more important to be able to ask your own computer to bring information from some outside database selectively, and process some of the results with internally generated data. The U.S. census tapes, for example, are available on several time-sharing databases. These can be used with in-company information to build a corporate model for facilities, for marketing, or for some other specific purpose.

Corporate models are still rudimentary, but progress in this area is expected to be very promising in the next few years. You will have more luck building your own with a time-sharing terminal than is likely with even the most eminent econometrists from outside because this kind of model in particular depends on intuitive understanding of the relationships and interactions within an organization. The effects of external economic factors, more generally understood, are often built in to these modeling languages that are available in business English from time-sharing services or software houses.

Once you begin to think about one of your files as a database, you begin edging into the Database Management business—another kind of diversification, but often a necessary one. It is interesting to note that a database *manager,* in today's terminology, is a computer program, while a database *administrator* is a person. Before you get too enmeshed in the subject, it is sensible to have an information director as well. The database administrator will have his hands quite full simply sorting out the different names your computer people and user departments have for exactly the same things, and keeping up with their needs to list these in different order. The information director can be the one who translates management requests for information into technical terms, determines their cost and feasibility, channels them through the proper systems, sets up the necessary OR or O and M groups to answer some of them, and differentiates between information and data throughout the company. The information director is also the one who can siphon out the extraneous three-inch reports, flowery fruits of creativity that computer people sometimes present to top management in the name of individual initiative.

The database administrator is the man who decides how data is to be related and handled; the information director should be the one to decide which data is needed in the system in order to keep real information flowing out of it. His basic job is to supervise the use of one of your most important and expensive corporate resources—information. Thus he should probably report at the same level as the finance director or production director—men who watch over the use of other corporate resources.

The file structure—the way in which the data is organized inside each file—requires a great deal of thought for successful use of your databases. This is particularly true in larger companies where identical information is often filed in wildly different categories from one division to another. The same item (say the junior engineer's hourly wage rate) can be variously called *wage rate, engineering expense, labor content item K, Jones, junior engineer,* and so on, in different files. It may be more or less retrievable according to how deeply it is embedded in the files. Sorting out just the nomenclature takes the wisdom of Job. Then deciding which files contain the latest junior engineering hourly wage is yet another major decision. This name-game from one department to another is common even in smaller companies, but seldom visible to top management because reports are presented in the jargon of the requester whenever possible. An information director or database administrator can sometimes help by creating a thesaurus of item names and insisting that no other items can be filed without having their names entered in the thesaurus.

One standardization group, Codasyl, has come up with a proposal for a standardized system for data management. Like any other standardized system, it has some limitations that will make it inconvenient in special cases. This Codasyl proposal is based on one language to define the relationships between different types of data or files, and another language (mostly a set of verbs such as *fetch* or *insert* that sound like instructions to a well-trained dog) to tell the system what you want once your information is organized. The structure is fairly complicated, but it makes sense. There is first of all an overall description or "schema" that outlines the primary purpose of the database. Various "subschema" then describe how this is accomplished in various computer languages. They are interpreted differently for the same languages in computers from different manufacturers (no two FORTRANS are alike), but the existence of the schema and subschema can make the resulting database management systems more transferable, and thus more useful and economical. The Codasyl group is primarily concerned with COBOL, so the first implementations are being done in that language. Univac is already working on a generalized COBOL version for its large 1100 series computers, but IBM registered major technical differences of opinion, so any standardization will be achieved in house-to-house guerrilla combat rather than one sweeping advance of well-ordered armies of computer people.

Even so, the Codasyl work provides a sound basis to begin planning for databases. (Copies of the latest reports of the Codasyl Database Task Group are available at negligible cost from the Association for Computing Machinery in New York City or the British Computer Society in London.) This structure can give your own systems analysts tools to begin creating their own system, yet one that could later grow onto other computers that come equipped with such a language for database handling. A number of companies have already used Codasyl's reports in this manner and say that they have been helpful.

Start slow. To get a database off the ground, you need five years of experience on the part of the people using that database. The technology exists today: the computers to shuffle the data, the mass storage systems to hold it, even the systems analysts to get it in fairly efficiently. But until all the people who use the data really know their way around an existing database, it won't be practical to confuse and upset them with more grandiose and complicated systems. If you plan the system from the top down, it will be possible to implement it in smaller chunks from the bottom up.

Once the overall structure for a beginning-level database has been decided and the system set up for describing the relationships between different kinds of files, then the donkey work begins: transferring the mountains of data into the computer files. Here, too, it makes sense to go slowly, in sensible order, rather than try to do everything at once. Some kinds of files may already be available in computer-readable form. These may need the format and order changed to fit your database plans. It may be possible to input some files by means of optical character reading equipment, but this is still fairly limited in the kinds of printing it can read.

Many files will simply have to be keypunched. Service bureaus can make this process less painful if you have a clear specification for exactly what you want.

THE CORPORATE INFORMATION SYSTEM

You have hired an information director and a database administrator. Between them they have worked with your user departments to design a flexible and workable file structure, one that describes the desired relationships between different kinds of data, leaving room for new relationships and new files or records. They have turned out a useful thesaurus that is being used throughout the company, even for noncomputerized files. Then they have gone through the drudgery of getting the files into the computer, or different computers for different departments, as the case may be.

Since MIS has come into disrepute, it might be wiser to call the result an embryonic corporate information system. Although the structure and thesaurus had to be designed to accommodate all the present and future needs of all departments, the sensible information director will probably concentrate on one portion of the system first. This first part of the system will undoubtedly encounter more procedural and human difficulties than all the others put together. Then he will bring up the other elements months or years later as people get used to using and trusting the first.

A classic corporate information system may consist of the following elements, though their nomenclature may differ:

> personnel information system
> financial information system
> marketing information system
> production information system

Where do you start? The insistence or reluctance of pertinent directors is always a major factor in the decision. The financial data is probably easiest to computerize because much of it is already in computer-readable form. Furthermore, many of the questions managers want to ask can be handled in financial terms. On the other hand, the highest payoff probably comes when the production system is running smoothly, with better inventory levels and deliveries, and some chance for full-scale production control. But Marketing is demanding an immediate tool to analyze all its sales for the past five years, and Personnel is threatening to buy a computer of its own. Or you may encounter the reverse situation, where independent directors will go to great lengths to keep anyone from fooling around with the procedures of their autonomous groups.

Parallel running with existing systems is one polite way to overcome this kind of reluctance. It is also a sensible safety plan. But parallel running can be a problem if you have highly dynamic files. Then it becomes a tough task, and an expensive one. Even so, this is the only way to make the change. Temporary staff can help tide you over the peak load of the parallel running until the new system has proved itself. Implementing in even smaller increments for such systems can also help.

One book company, part of a large publishing organization, went along to a few computer planning meetings at which it was announced that they would have a new automated warehousing and invoicing system on a certain June first, some months away. They did not attend several later planning meetings, at which it was revealed there might be some delay. On the appointed day, all the ordering and invoicing people for the manual system were given their severance pay and sent home. The computer system was two weeks late, so the people had to be called back immediately. Then, as soon as all the book and subscription orders for Christmas had been irrevocably entered into the computer system, it crashed. (This was in the sixties, when automation accidents were a little more frequent than they are today.) The manual people were called back once again to try to sort things out, but at least $1.2 million worth of books had been shipped without any records remaining of the shipments. Letters (noncomputerized) were finally sent out to all customers, saying in essence: "We are having computer troubles, so we don't quite know what we have sent you. Would you please send us what you think you owe?" It is a pleasant commentary on business honesty that the eventual loss was slightly under $250,000. The computer was working properly by Christmas.

The cost of parallel running for several weeks or even months is negligible compared with this kind of mess. If you are converting from manual systems, it is also wise to staff the new system as much as possible with people from the old one—people who will have a better understanding of how the department itself really works. Most people respond with enthusiasm to a chance to learn computing, while the ones who do not choose to move may find new career paths within the department as others move.

SECURITY FOR DATABASES

Information is an important corporate resource. It is getting more concentrated in computer rooms. The databases that are used to generate information deserve as much protection against fire, theft, acts of God, and disgruntled individuals as your warehouses or your cash. Yet some companies still store their "grandfather tapes" and "father tapes" in the same room as their latest-generation updated tapes. This risks destruction of the entire database. Fireproof vaults for tapes or disks are available and used in many companies. Yet they usually stand open all day, and sometimes all night.

An article in *Datamation*[3] listed four new worries for managers who keep their data in computers:

1. Accidental or inadvertent damage or destruction of software, hardware, or stored data.
2. Malicious damage to or destruction of software, hardware, or stored data.
3. Theft or fraud which deprives an organization of physical assets.
4. Theft of private or classified information.

A backup system can make the difference between success and failure if something awful happens to your computer. It can also be convenient and reassuring in a minor crisis or overload. Large companies that centralize their computing are leaning toward having several centers with identical computer systems, rather than one monster center with the two computers back-to-back. Data communications makes this easy. For smaller companies it makes sense to know which bureaus can run your particular jobs verbatim—most common computer configurations can be matched or bettered by a convenient bureau. If you insist on having the only Bloggs computer in commercial use in Kansas, make sure Bloggs can and will support you with one of its own computers for backup.

Theft and sabotage horror stories are getting more common. There's

3. "Security of Computer-Based Information Systems," W. S. Bates, *Datamation*, May 1970.

the bank programmer in Britain who had the computer put all leftover halfpennies into his own account when it computed the new decimalized values for everyone else. Another apocryphal story that has come true several times (probably because of the existence of the apocryphal story) deals with the personnel programmer who made his own employee number the security key for his company's payroll program, so it would never run unless his number were on the roster. An 1108 computer at one bureau in California was able to dial up and switch a key program from a competitor's 1108 across the bay (thanks to a customer who insisted on having the same password on both systems "for convenience"). The bureau knew nothing about this activity, but an enterprising programmer (who was eventually brought to court) thought he could start a competing service with the program. Few accountants could uncover, trace, or evaluate the loss involved in such intrusions.

Never underestimate the cleverness of a highly motivated individual. An experiment at Massachusetts Institute of Technology (which has one of the world's earliest and most advanced time-sharing systems) offered free computer time to students who could break the security codes of other students. Even more free computer time was awarded to any who could devise unbreakable security measures on the time-sharing system. Every single security system was broken within a few months.

The use of terminal systems inside companies, as well as bureau systems where people from many companies can access a single computer, is growing almost as rapidly as companies are putting their most essential and private information into computers. No security system is foolproof, but there are steps that can help terminal users:

> Not only should each terminal have its own identification signal, but each user should have his own access code.

> Programs stored in computers, especially bureau computers, should be keyed so they can be used only by approved users, working from approved terminals.

> Furthermore, the program and access codes should be easily changeable (by one or two trusted managers), and should be changed often —at least every time a concerned employee leaves the company. Some companies change access codes every week.

An on-line terminal, unattended but already connected to its computer, is a strong temptation for potential information thieves. Particularly if you have a general information system working on line, make sure terminals are never unattended, and give special access codes for the requests for the most private information.

Security for data should be part of the training program for all computer staff and all staff in user departments who have anything to do with the computer. There should also be competent successors trained for key posts, so you're not left with a mess of undocumented pottage if the chief programmer is lured away—one of the worst and most common kinds of corporate sabotage.

Internal information pilferage is a much more common occurrence than most top managers realize. This is a major worry for the middle managers who direct the activities of competitive groups inside a company. Particularly in corporations that have autonomous product-oriented groups, intramural competition is common. Internal and even external time-sharing systems tend to be used with simply a department number as the access key or the suffix to the generally known access key. This means that the curious employee in the widgets division only needs to plug in the number for the nuts and bolts division, asking questions in the approved format, to know all N and B's sales for the past quarter and its projections for the next quarter—or worse yet, its plans for taking 5000 square feet presently being used by Widgets. This kind of leakage may be less harmful than outside theft to the corporation as a whole, but it will eventually drive the nuts and bolts manager back to manual systems, no matter what the consequences. Or he will store false information, which biases and cuts the usefulness of the entire information system.

Computer theft or sabotage are fearsome prospects, but there are sensible measures that can help. Your database is a crucial corporate resource, yet you would never know whether it had been stolen or not. The loyalty of your people is your first line of protection—and computer people are so often treated as foreign eggheads that they tend to be more loyal to the computer manufacturer than their employers. Goal-oriented management, avenues for advancement beyond the computer realm, and some sort of profit-sharing approach that involves them in the success of the company can make some difference in this attitude. The people who are allowed into your data center are all able to do potential damage or steal data. Make sure you have a receptionist or other guardian of the doors, and make particularly sure this person is not vulnerable to a bribe from a competitor. Separate (and locked) storage places for the grandfather tapes and disks can help you recoup if a discharged operator chooses to flit through the current storage section with the apocryphal magnet in his hand.

Separating the programming and operation of the computer helps security, and also saves money because programmers won't tie up the entire system looking for a bug in a single program. They will be forced to write clearer operating instructions for their programs, and won't make as many extra runs. They're also less likely to indulge in games or fraud in their programs when they know a separate operator will be watching the results. Programming from a time-sharing terminal sidesteps this issue; access codes should usually be limited to the project presently under development.

Written specifications reviewed before programs are written, standards for approved programming techniques, and an insistence on complete documentation, general enough for managers to understand and techical enough for someone else to be able to amend the programs, can save months of rework and eliminate temptation for programmers who might otherwise work in solitary splendor. If proper flow charts are used, it is possible to test every path of a program with sample batches of real data as well as artificial "worst case" test data.

Key files (such as lists of accounts receivable) can be protected from complete theft by imposing the slightly awkward requirement that they be partitioned onto more than one tape or disk or printout. This way, though one portion may be filched, duplicated, or lost, the probability of losing the entire file is considerably less. The requirement also makes the people handling such company confidential information more security conscious. So does the formation of a security steering committee, preferably including the company's auditor and the external computer auditor.

If the computer logs everything it does and you have proper control procedures for operators, you are less likely to find that a copy of your financial tape has found its way into your competitors' hands. Industrial espionage has been more popular in the United States than in Europe; janitorial services, for example, are sometimes involved in cloak-and-dagger activities. At least one in California (and probably several dozen) regularly retrieve from trash cans the important printouts, discarded computer tapes, or even carbon typewriter ribbons that might blunt a competitive edge. Marketing departments are usually key targets for this kind of spying. Most of the information theft suffered in every country comes from people inside the installation, not outsiders. BOAC discovered a few years ago that its $100 million seat reservation system was being offered for sale to other airlines—by a few renegade members of the BOAC staff. Once the crucial information was known to be in the public domain, BOAC itself simply went into the business of selling the system to other airlines.

It is possible to set up control systems as complicated as those that govern military missiles: duplicate control consoles, full-time security watches by independent experts, two or three separate keys or codes in the custody of different people before the system can be turned on. None of these is foolproof. There are at least two things any company *can* do that will cut the chance and cost of data theft, sabotage, or loss:

Keep grandfather files locked in fireproof vaults, preferably located away from the computer.

Make sure computer-related employees see their own achievement and progress related closely to the success of your company.

A number of alarming but useful articles dealing with security in the computer room have been published in the past few years. Here's a multi-national sampling:

"Danger Ahead! Safeguard Your Computer," Brandt Allen, *Harvard Business Review,* November-December 1968, Cambridge, Mass.

"Is This the Perfect Crime?," Brian Moynahan, *Sunday Times,* 7 March 1971, London, England.

"Keeping Computers Safe," G. F. Parker, *Management Today,* September 1969, London, England.

"Security & the Computer," L. H. Fine, *The South African Chartered Accountant,* September 1970, Johannesburg, South Africa.

"Some Legal Aspects of Commercial Remote Access Computer Services," R. P. Bigelow, *Datamation,* August 1969, Pasadena, California.

7

Auditing the Computer Itself

When you buy a new car, you get with it a schedule for maintenance and tune-ups: 1000 miles, 5000 miles, 10,000 miles, all the way up to 100,000 miles or more—if you're lucky, and you've had a good mechanic.

The computer requires similar maintenance and tuning up, for more than just the machinery. When a manufacturer installs a computer, he also gives you a recommended maintenance schedule. In the emergency crashes and repairs that used to characterize new installations, these schedules were sometimes overlooked, but they are generally sensible. Nobody knows better than the maker which parts of the machine are likely to give trouble.

Whether this maintenance was done by the manufacturer or by the sophisticated user himself, it usually dealt only with the computer hardware. The real benefits in tuning up a system come when the entire conglomeration of hardware, software, and people is checked over carefully at regular intervals—by independent experts.

This is called the computer audit. The name is both limiting and misleading, but its use is widespread. Accountants use the term to refer to the audit of a company's books in which the computer is used as an aid to the classic auditor. This might better be termed the *computer-assisted audit*. When we refer to the review of the entire EDP function itself as a "computer audit," there is a tendency to think only of the computer and the people in the DP room. The phrase *computer-management audit* describes the 10,000-mile checkup more accurately. Figure 7-1 shows the interacting elements that must be taken into consideration when this kind of audit is done.

MEASURING EFFICIENCY

It is now possible to measure the performance of computer hardware fairly accurately. There are machines, software, and consulting services that can be used to give a measure of throughput. These are useful in their place—as a small part of the computer audit.

They are also dangerous. They encourage the "instructions-per-minute syndrome," a racetrack approach to DP management. "I get more ipm out of my computer than you get out of your computer" belongs in the playroom, not the board room. It is seldom synonymous with: "I run the

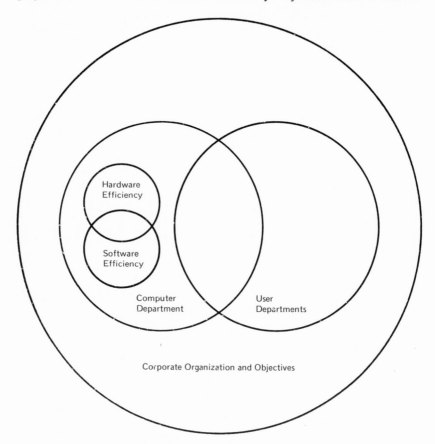

Fig. 7-1. Venn diagram for a computer audit. The universal set is the corporation, not the computer.

most effective DP installation in town." The appropriateness of the applications is a much better measure of the computer's real usefulness.

It is also possible to measure the efficiency of software. There are no plug-in machines to do this, but benchmark programs and good test data, used by experienced consultants, can give a valid indication of how tightly programs are written. This, too, is a useful tool for the computer auditor, although the changing cost of storage may make tight programming less important to overall efficiency in some applications. But this kind of measurement is also expensive, and probably worthwhile only for frequently used applications or systems software.

Benchmark programs, which exercise the different parts of a system in a known pattern, can also be used to look at hardware performance. They are most useful for comparing different makes and configurations of computers, especially if they match your own particular mix of processing tasks. Most manufacturers are happy to furnish benchmark programs, at little or no cost. Not surprisingly, these benchmarks usually reveal that the donor's system is the most efficient. The computer auditor normally uses independently developed benchmarks if he needs any at all. In large installations it may be worthwhile developing a few of your own that represent your particular mix of operations. However, benchmarks are often overrated.

Programmer efficiency can also be measured. Statements-per-day is as misleading a measure of efficiency as instructions-per-minute. Nonetheless, an understanding of programming standards can help a consultant evaluate the programmer output for quantity as well as quality. So does his view of the average performance in comparable installations. For do-it-yourself evaluation, several simple programs are now available commercially to keep track of the progress of programming projects on a sensible sub-project and task basis. Used over a period of time, these can give a useful comparison of the output (and effectiveness) of different programmers doing similar tasks.

Some consulting firms specialize in writing programming standards for their clients, then training programmers in their use. These standards define to varying levels the logic, the languages, and the specific methods to be used in writing programs within that installation. They can also describe standard data structures for all installations and departments in a larger company. Engineering the consent of the governed is often the most critical step in implementing such standards. Properly used, they can also be training tools that permit a company to create its own programmers from within.

Standards sometimes tell how to break programming projects into subprojects and modules that can be written and checked out individually, then put together in different ways. Standardized interfaces between the modules are defined in the standards, so they fit together like pieces in a puzzle. There are also special languages such as AED (sponsored by the U.S. Air Force and supported by Softech, Inc., in Waltham, Mass.), which are particularly designed for modular programming. Bringing standards for modular programming into an installation, especially one with a high programmer population, can result in a drastic improvement in efficiency. Less experienced (and thus less expensive) programmers can be used to write the various modules, while the expensive senior people spend more of their time designing the puzzle itself rather than the individual pieces. Modules, once written and debugged, tend to stay bug-free, and can be used again and again in other programs.

Modular programming often brings with it one particular management problem. The programmers, like any other threatened group of employees, tend to resist any attempt to automate their jobs. Unless the introduction of the standards carries with it the promise of more interesting work, many of them will find subtle or unsubtle ways of obstructing the project. Several companies have sidestepped such staff problems by putting key programmers into teams with the standards experts to amend the off-the-shelf standards to the particular needs and practices of the installation or corporation.

ORGANIZING THE AUDIT

Measuring and reporting on the efficiency of hardware, software, and programmers do *not* constitute a complete audit of the DP function. People are the crucial part of the overall system. The largest improvements usually come at the strategic level. For this reason, the auditor should be a man who can look at the entire organization and the interactions between various elements within it. He must be able to ask whether the computer is being used for the right work, in addition to finding out how fast it is churning out the work.

Choosing an auditor for your computing is like choosing a doctor for your family. You are inviting him into your company to look at the most intimate details of day-to-day operation and to report on relationships that affect the overall strategy of the company. In addition to having complete confidence in his technical and management judgment, you must be able to trust him—to guard your corporate secrets as your doctor guards confidential information about your health. You must also respect him enough to listen to sometimes unpleasant observations about the way the company and the computer department interact.

Peter Drucker points out that secret reporting is seldom the best way for a consultant to work within an organization. The most successful auditors are usually those who are highly oriented to the line managers and DP managers rather than to their board-level bosses. Understanding and sympathizing with middle-management problems, such auditors can make it clear that they share the goal of improving the operation. (Granted, the task of finding a gem who can empathize with middle management at the same time that he views the strategic elements with a top-management eye is seldom easy.) In this atmosphere, minor changes can sometimes be suggested verbally and implemented instantly, then reported in a commendatory tone to top management. The secret "spy report" is normally less effective than one that has been reviewed with each manager who was concerned in the audit. Because the cooperation of the middle managers is essential to the success of the audit—and any proposed changes resulting from it—this open attitude can make a major difference.

The first step in the audit is to establish the terms of reference between the consultant and the company. These terms define the start and finish points, the depth to which different aspects will be studied, the limitations to the study, and the specific and general problems and objectives. The most effective audits occur when the company management, the consultant, and the employees all understand what will be done and why.

Project control for the audit itself can be an example of the measurement and control that are being studied. It can also save you money. The client and consultant should agree about how information will feed through their respective organizations during the audit. There must be a mechanism for increasing the auditor's attention to newly discovered problem areas or cutting off consultant concentration in portions of the company that are running smoothly—or impossibly.

Don't give the auditor a blank check, or an open-ended contract. If major attention is needed in certain areas, this should be beyond the scope of the audit. Instead, it should come in the form of a separate contract, subject to its own selection criteria and negotiation. The best auditors are not always the best implementers, and vice versa.

The computer audit is analogous to the corporate financial audit in many ways, and the computer auditor is reviewing computer-related systems like the company auditor reviews conventional systems. Perhaps because of differences in legal and banking requirements, this concept of auditing seems to have evolved to a slightly higher level in Europe than it is in the United States. Similarly, I have seen more European companies that understand the concept of an audit trail when it applies to computer activities, though I am quite willing to be proved wrong.

Like an accounting audit, the computer audit is really a series of questions. When these are answered, checked, and cross-checked as much as possible, they should give the auditor and corporate management a three-dimensional picture of the company's data processing operations, highlighting places where savings can be made or problems are likely to occur.

AUDIT CHECKLIST

Different auditors have different ways of approaching the task, but nearly all of them have detailed checklists. These are sometimes highly secret tomes that run to 100 pages or more. The client deserves to have his own list of what the auditor is going to look for. He should also have a chance to veto certain portions of the audit. If there has been an impenetrable brick wall between the manufacturing manager and the DP manager for the past ten years, there's no need to pay an auditor to tell you so, unless he can suggest sensible ways of breaching it. A separate study of DP and manufacturing (or some expert assistance in knocking heads together at the boundary) is more likely to be fruitful.

Most auditors start by collecting mountains of existing information such as organization charts, flow charts, copies of programs and logs. Then they come into the company with their checklists to clean up these installation statistics, exploring discrepancies or distortions and looking at management aspects of the operation that cannot possibly reveal themselves on paper.

The following summary is a composite of the questions a number of reputable computer auditors say they try to answer:

Organization

How does the computer organization fit within the company? Is it suitably placed to interface with user departments? Does the DP department "sell" its services? Does DP operate on the same profit-and-loss basis as other elements of the company?

How does DP mesh with management services, Organization and Methods, operations research, corporate modeling, or finance?

Where are the chains of command? Where do practical relationships differ from the organization chart? Does the structure permit efficient decision making?

Who ultimately controls the DP department? Is there a steering committee?

Are responsibilities defined and understood, both within the DP department and with respect to other departments?

Is DP central to corporate activity, or out on the fringe?

Are relationships between the DP manager and other managers on a sound basis? This part of the audit often includes a survey of managers in user departments, who also contribute information about applications and other aspects. One key result of the organization study can be an unbiased evaluation of intracompany communications.

Forward Planning

Is there a forward plan for DP? How far ahead does it go?

Does the plan include career development?

Does the DP department have the resources (people, money, machines, and management) to meet its forward plan?

Has the plan been approved by corporate management?

Is DP aware of corporate planning?

Is the computer used for corporate forecasting? Should it be?

Do user departments have forward plans that include DP? Do they mesh with the DP plan, or is DP going a separate direction?

How well do present and projected workloads fit the plans?

Where will the inevitable bottlenecks occur? Have they been anticipated?

DP Management

Is DP management familiar with company objectives? How loyal are managers and technical people?

How effective are managers and technical people?

How are they selected and trained?

How is morale in the DP department?

Do job descriptions exist?

What are staff turnover rates?

Is the size of the staff consistent with the workload?

Is salary policy consistent with others in the same industry?

Are comparisons made between current and previous costs and forecasts? Are these related to company turnover and other indicators?

Are comparisons made between current internal performance versus costs for such external alternatives as bureaus or reverting to manual handling for some applications?

How are systems projects controlled?

How efficient is the use of men, money, and machines?

How are peaks handled? Are these forced on the DP department by users or are they self-generated? Can the configuration cope with peaks? Should it?

Are there standards for systems analysis, design, programming, program maintenance, quality control, documentation, or service to users?

User Departments

What kind of service do users think they are getting?

Do they understand the constraints of the DP operation? How do they view the DP department?

Do they use the reports that they get?

What are their attitudes to various applications programs? (These responses can be checked against program maintenance logs to reveal biases and discrepancies.)

Do they give and get easy-to-understand specifications?

Are clerical instructions clear?

Do users impose reasonable deadlines and reporting requirements?

How involved have they been in the design of their applications? Did they take part in the systems analysis, or did the DP department encounter obstructions, or ignore them? If so, why?

The Applications

How are priorities determined for applications programming?

How are programming and operating costs charged to users? How do these charges relate to actual costs?

How do final costs compare with original estimates and justifications? Were ten clerks actually saved? (If so, what happened to them?) Is the company or the DP department routinely carrying out similar checks?

Are the applications programs presently being used? What is the planned versus the actual frequency of input? Are programs out of date? A quick listing of seldom-used applications is often revealing.

Are off-the-shelf packages used?

Can applications be standardized for use in different departments?

Programming

Are applications programmed efficiently? If table look-up is not performed in a binary search manner, for example, it can make the difference between one hour and only three minutes running time for a given application on a 360/50.

How (and by whom) is the programming language chosen or perpetuated? Some companies that used to use FORTRAN in some departments and COBOL in others are now standardizing on PL/1, for example.

What do the programming specifications look like?

What standards are used?

Are testing procedures satisfactory?

Equipment

Are hardware costs reasonable?

How often does hardware break down?

Is it possible to sort out which reruns are due to hardware, software, or programmer error? Are rerun times acceptable? How much is charged for extra time?

Are standby facilities available?

When does maintenance take place?

How well does the manufacturer support the installation? How do manufacturer people relate to DP staff? It is sometimes interesting to compare the manufacturer's original specification for the equipment required to handle the workload with the actual configuration (and workload) that has grown up.

Are hardware and overhead costs in line with each other?

What about media and forms? Simple changes like a one-part paper versus a six-part paper can sometimes bring substantial savings.

Is new hardware required to meet planned growth?

Job Scheduling

What determines priorities?

How detailed and effective is daily scheduling?

What kinds of records are kept?

How is the tape library organized?

How is job stacking done?

Operating

How clear and comprehensive are the operating instructions?

How is control maintained?

Are operators conscious of security for data?

How do operators liaise with programmers? Are they encouraged to learn programming?

Does the operation achieve minimum setup time? Does it have procedures to know how one operator compares with another in this respect?

Do staff members make optimum use of the equipment? Internal logs can be checked to assure that they are being kept properly and to cross-check the standard of operating efficiency.

Data Preparation

How legible are source documents?

How is editing carried out?

How does data get from the point of origin into the computer?

What determines batch sizes?

How are errors dealt with?

What controls exist?

Are there standards for data preparation people?

How are data preparation services charged?

Housekeeping

Is space adequate?

What is the flow of work?

Where are tapes or disks kept?

Where are jobs stacked?

Do staff members have reasonable working conditions?

Can supervisors see what is happening?

Do controls exist to prevent unauthorized visitors?

Do housekeeping standards protect machines, tapes, disks, and other media?

Bookkeeping

Do audit trails exist? Do they follow normal accounting practice?

What controls exist for the accuracy of input and output?

How often are financial reports demanded? How often are they needed?

Does vital information get "lost" in the DP department for too long? Are some functions being handled manually for this reason?

Does the DP department budget include cost appreciation?

Are programs accounted for as corporate assets? How are they depreciated?

FINDING AN AUDITOR

Neither an ear-nose-throat specialist nor a nurse is qualified to carry out a complete medical checkup. To return to the car analogy, you wouldn't necessarily ask the man who repairs the dent in the door to tune the engine. The computer audit also calls for a specialist. With questions spanning the entire operation of the company, credentials for software alone or management consulting alone seldom suffice for the computer audit.

Some management consultant firms and accounting firms have developed competent EDP teams in the past few years. Others have thrown themselves and their clients into very hot water indeed by assuming that EDP can be evaluated without direct experience in the field.

A few software houses have acquired corporate-level management consulting capability. But it is best to remember that the majority are made up of programmers, whose entire experience revolves around the computer. Without direct management experience in the client's industry, they are unlikely to be able to evaluate the subtle corporate relationships and requirements that often make the difference between success and failure in the use of the computer.

The exceptions in both the computer and management consulting fields are growing into a new class—the strategic-level computer consultants. A few of these are individuals who combine all the needed skills for an audit. The majority are large enough to be able to call on specialists for different aspects of the audit. It is false economy to use less than first-class people when you are buying professional advice. The best seldom cost more, but the amount they can save you could be enormous.

Armed with a handy list for doing a computer audit, the user sometimes decides to save money and conduct his own. But just as doctors never treat themselves or their own families, companies should bring in outside experts for this job. If you do it yourself, you are unlikely to see some of the possible improvements simply because the traditional way of doing things is comfortable and familiar. An unbiased outside view is worth the expense, particularly in this area. So is the experience the auditor has gained in a number of similar companies.

Another pitfall for the unwary is the free audit. This is sometimes offered by a software house or consulting firm. Not often. Computer manufacturers also have been known to offer very-low-cost or free audits. This is usually another name for a sales visit. The result is likely to be a recommendation for lots of new equipment. Unless you are really in the market for a new computer and your people are willing to put up with intrusive salesmen in order to have two or three competitive "audits" in lieu of proposals from the manufacturers, it is probably best to refuse the free audit. You usually get exactly what you pay for.

A NEW COMPUTER?

The audit can sometimes save the cost of a new computer. In the earlier days of computing, consultants were accustomed to designing new systems or applications and helping their clients specify new equipment. In this context, an audit usually resulted in recommendations for new expenditures because expansion was the basic reason for outgrowing the old system and calling in the consultants.

Consultants have had more trouble than many of their clients have had in getting used to the new climate in computing. Many are still challenged most by the opportunity to create something new. Even so, most of them see that making savings for their clients is today's path to consulting survival.

Computer sales are not rising as fast as computer use. This means that many second- and even third-generation computers are becoming overloaded. Like traffic on a freeway as the rush hour approaches, two or three new applications threaten to bring the entire system screeching to a halt.

A new computer is *not* always the best answer. We live in a volatile business world. Applications change every day. Mergers, acquisitions, or new products shift the focus of a company. Different portions change at different rates. The risk of freezing yourself into outmoded procedures rises as the rate of change increases.

Before you give up and order the new computer, with all the reprogramming, retraining, and refinancing it will demand, call in the computer auditor. Give him special instructions to concentrate on culling out old applications and streamlining operations so that the computing traffic will flow smoothly for several more years. He may find that an investment of X to reprogram a few frequently used applications so that they run faster or store more tidily can free the computer for Y hours a week. If the traffic jam is concentrated in the storage area, he may be able to find masses of data that can be off-loaded onto other media. Some problem projects may be allowed to expire gracefully before they're finished, freeing people for more important work. Other projects may be worth more vigorous attention.

Facilities management is sometimes recommended when a system running on one or two shifts a day has reached saturation. This is discussed in detail in Chapter 9. In a sense, the facilities management company simply does its own audit and then gets the benefits of implementing the improvements instead of just recommending them.

The economics of bureau use are changing, and the range of choices available in most cities is improving rapidly. In some installations a medium-size computer can actually be replaced with a remote-batch terminal to a big bureau computer. In other companies, audits can reveal applications such as payroll that can be done for a lower cost outside. Putting other applications into a bureau may be justified even when it costs a trifle more if it adds several years to the life of a workable in-house computer configuration.

Some financial forecasting and resource allocation can now be done directly by accounting and planning people on time-sharing terminals. This can relieve the DP department of elaborate and expensive programming and systems design jobs, in fields that otherwise require special knowledge.

In many installations, a careful audit and review of application costs and historical justifications may show applications that ought to revert to manual handling. Inventory control, for example, has been a fashionable computer application for some years. The benefits, however, do not always justify the cost. Some companies are reverting to manual methods, while others turn to on-line bureaus for inventory control. These can sometimes handle up to a few thousand items of stock with inquiries from inexpensive Teletype-type terminals at many remote locations. This also has the merit of up-to-date answers, returned instantly—if you need the information that fast.

If all else fails and the system is still headed for a major traffic jam, the auditor may recommend adding secondhand equipment that matches the present configuration. There is a brisk and growing market in used computers (see Chapter 10). Though the older-generation machines lack glamour, they work. They also cost less. Operations can continue virtually unchanged. There's no training or reprogramming.

The possibilities are numerous. The important thing is to let the auditor develop realistic grounds for your decision. This means keeping track of costs for existing and potential applications. Thus you can see which are justified on an in-house system and how they measure up against the various alternatives.

If you really *do* need a new computer, the audit is still a healthy exercise to carry out before the decision is made. The new machines are generally more cost effective than their predecessors. You will certainly gain a clearer idea of your particular mix of job types. With careful specifying and a cleaned-up list of applications, you may end up paying less than you do for the present machine—a trend that is beginning to worry the computer manufacturers. Most of the new machines are supposed to accommodate some of the preceding generation's programs, though this is seldom as easy or inexpensive as it sounds; it's another area where the auditor can help.

WHEN TO CALL IN THE AUDITOR

It is perfectly possible to get in a state of EDP hypochondria—the absurd situation of overauditing a system. Usually this results in under-improving it. Like your children, your computers generally thrive on a regime of careful basic attention combined with healthy surface neglect. If clouds of consultants and auditors are constantly wafting over the DP installation, they will be resented and finally taken for granted. Their reports will simply exacerbate the paper-proliferation problem. Real work will be interrupted. Management will tend to contrast and query the different recommendations, rather than implementing them—like over-solicitous parents shunting their slow-reading child from school to school so fast he can't master word-pictures *or* phonics. Too many consultants also cost too much. It's usually better to find one computer-doctor you trust and stay with him.

Common sense says your car should have a good safety checkup at least once a year. Medical checkups are recommended on an annual basis. The computer also benefits from an annual review. This is frequent enough to keep people on their toes and catch sloppy programming or procedures before they become ingrained. Yet it is rare enough that the audit becomes an important event. If the consultant is also the sort who can be used for other strategic-level tasks, he will have additional chances to gain the confidence of the staff and managers.

The auditor often unconsciously points up problems in an organization like a painter touching up hairline cracks in a wall. When the computer room is all painted, with its procedures polished and its organization enameled, the drastic improvement is likely to highlight the run-down condition of adjacent organizations, starting a never-ending chain of repairs and redecoration. These are top-management matters, and should no more be left to the consultant than should the housewife's redecorating job be left to her painter.

Because organizations are interconnected in subtle and delicate ways, it is sensible to go very slowly in making even the smallest changes. One large banking company had major problems when it installed a modern, multiprogramming computer to handle computing for the entire corporation. Previously, one department had an IBM 1401 of its own, and that, in turn, had been preceded by a punched card system. Because each change of equipment took place in a crisis atmosphere, with simple translation or emulation of the foregoing programs, the modern time-sharing machine was not only being run like a card system, it was causing major interdepartmental battles. The new computer department, still staffed by people from the preceding era, suffered high staff turnover, nervous breakdowns, computer breakdowns, and organizational breakdowns. The department that had owned the previous machine was alarmed at deterioration in the quality of the service. Other departments, on the other hand, could see the former computer-owners getting preferential treatment on what they thought was to be *their* computer. Tempers were short and deadlines were often missed, while costs shot up and many departments resorted to bureau services.

When a new computer manager was hired, the bank called in consultants for a quick audit, to give him a "snapshot" of the situation at his arrival. "We were critically short of the kind of staff we needed," he later commented. "We were also lurching from crisis to crisis, with no time to stand back and find out where we stood and do some planning. The consultants were able to help overnight with the staffing problems, and give us the breathing space we needed to see how to tidy things up."

The audit revealed many small, unexpected improvements that could be made quickly. Even these were carefully screened for their effect on people before they were implemented. The quickest and most important change was the edict that no orders could thenceforth be taken verbally by the computer department. While the audit was going on, the computer manager worked with other departments and with the consultants to create a document that spelled out in detail the procedures for getting new applications onto the computer. This document was circulated to all departments, fully discussed, and finally adhered to rigorously. It called for the set of meetings and written agreements described in detail in Chapter 5. "By going through a lengthy evaluation, discussing the application with everyone involved down to the postal clerk, we often took longer to implement an application than we used to," said the computer manager. "In one instance, it took two years for a major task, though we could have had a technical solution within six months. If we had followed that course, the inevitable result would have been disaster. This way, everyone knew exactly how they were affected by the new system, and it went up smoothly. The managers in the affected departments didn't want us talking to their people at first, but now the application is working, they're convinced."

Despite its complexity and the amount of experience the auditor must have, a computer audit need not be expensive. Several eminent consultants say the complete audit can take as little as two weeks, especially if they have been involved in previous planning, feasibility, or training tasks that have familiarized them with the organization. The first audit is likely to take longer because the consultant will need to spend more time learning the system and the structure of the company and collecting statistics. He will also have to unravel the intricacies of de facto as well as official relationships before he can fit the technical study inside its organizational framework.

It's worth the trouble. You get better mileage from a well-tuned computer department.

8

Leasing Versus Buying

Companies that provide cars for their key men often prefer to lease them. An accountant likes this because it doesn't tie up capital, and it gives him a simple lump sum for auto expenses to work with. The facilities man usually likes it, especially if maintenance is included in the contract, because if something goes wrong with your Rover, he can usually trade it back to the lessor and ask for another until it's fixed. Car makers rather like it because the sales are painless, though they might prefer to get more of the lucrative leasing business themselves.

The primary reason for leasing a computer is the same—you avoid tying up a lot of capital.

Most computer manufacturers set up their ratios of monthly rental to purchase price on the basis of something between 40:1 and 50:1. Most computer companies write off their machines on a three- to five-year basis, though a new series computer purchased at the beginning of its life is sometimes written off on a six-year basis. Users usually take longer write-off periods for purchased machines.

If you look around at the number of ten-year-old 1401 or 1130 computers in use (or the number of seven-year-old cars that were depreciated over three years), the profit and risk in leasing become quite clear.

GENESIS AND EXODUS OF COMPUTER LEASING

In the beginning all computers and big business machines were leased. As a company called International Business Machines, Inc. began to take

121

more and more of this business at different stages in the growth of the computer industry, the U.S. government decided this was sinful and threatened to break up the company because it was becoming a monopoly. Antitrust lawsuits were settled in 1936 and 1956. The current suit may drag on into the mid-seventies. In 1956 IBM and the Justice Department finally signed an agreement, the famous Consent Decree, which stipulated (among other things, including release of tightly held patents) that IBM would henceforth sell its computers as well as rent them. It also stipulated that IBM would put more distance between itself and its service bureau business, which was similarly approaching monopoly stature. This was the origin of Service Bureau Corporation in the United States. The dividing lines between the two are still unclear on occasion. IBM ran its own time-sharing services, Call/360 and Datatext, for several years, on the premise that time sharing was still in the development stages. For a year after Call/360 was officially shifted to SBC, most inquiries made to local SBC offices about time sharing were referred to IBM sales people.

Even in the fifties IBM held about 80 percent of the world market, so anything IBM did had a major impact on the other computer manufacturers. The changeover to a mixture of sales and leasing was as deliberate as the steps toward separate bureau services. Even so, the pattern developed inexorably, and the other computer companies adapted their own stances in relation to it.

The crux of the matter was to establish a proper relationship between computer manufacturers' sale and lease prices and their writeoff policies. The Justice Department had believed (with perhaps some justice) that there was considerable concern when lease prices were not pegged to visible purchase prices. When these finally settled down, IBM's internal writeoff policies were based on five-year straight-line calculations. GE opted for a more conservative five-year declining balance policy. Honeywell eventually chose a more adventurous six-year straight-line basis. The other manufacturers clustered around these levels in accordance with their own corporate personalities.

It wasn't until much closer to the 1960 mark that computers were familiar enough so that a few entrepreneurs began to do their sums and realize that the machines could be written off over longer time periods. Users seldom wrote off their purchased computers in less than eight years. If a computer could be depended on not only to work but to be rentable over ten years, then a six-year-old computer fully depreciated (by a manufacturer) still had four more income-producing years. There was a fairly large "if" built in to the equation in those days. Reliability was somewhat less than impressive in the early generations. The manufacturers tended to come out with new generations every six years. And users were notoriously faddish.

By 1958 a company called Boothe Leasing was beginning to go into computer leasing. Two of its alumni later formed Levin-Townsend, which made major strides in computer leasing. Another early company was Leasco, founded by a 21-year-old Wharton graduate named Saul Steinberg, after he had written a thesis based on IBM's approaches to finance. Though Leasco later specialized in IBM equipment, in its earliest days the company leased NCR accounting machines on a low-risk basis with full-payoff leases.

Entire industries have sprung up simply to fill chinks in IBM's marketing armor. The leasing industry, like the bureaus, enjoyed a certain inviolability because it was sure that the Justice Department would continue to watch over its chink. Most leasing companies bought computers and depreciated them over something like a ten-year period to a 10 percent residual value. They were able to put the machines out on three- to five-year leases comparable to those of the manufacturers, for about 25 percent per month less. A few of the early leasing companies chose even more grandiose write-off schemes.

It became an accountant's wonderland overnight; Wall Street was enchanted. Stock prices doubled, tripled, quadrupled in a few months or less. The over-the-counter investment market couldn't keep up with the demand for leasing stocks, so groups of business-school boys or young lawyers or computer salesmen set up shop in odd corners near Wall Street, dashed off to their banks for letters of credit (which were usually forthcoming), issued a few press releases, and floated their stock.

Revolving credit of $50 million or more from a conservative bank for such a fledgling company was not unusual during the earlier sixties. Leasing gobbled up amazing quantities of capital. "If we don't get in and cover Houston in a hurry, somebody else is going to set up shop there." In its first years, a typical leasing company turned over enormous quantities of other people's money, often with a staff of two and a half (the "half" being a moonlighter) doing the paper-shuffling in a loft in the nether regions of New York City. Stock values continued to skyrocket. Several of the maturing companies began to look around for their own continuing sources of capital. Continued stock appreciation required continued growth, which required a constant flow of new leases.

The cash-hungry leasing lads thought they had found their mates in troubled banks or insurance companies that had not quite kept up with the pace of the technological times. These matronly institutions often viewed their dynamic new fiancés with baffled and wary attitudes, but leasing stocks were still going up, and the offers could seldom be refused.

In addition to the constant need for cash, the leasing companies had two other pervasive worries. In the mid-sixties most of them had settled down to a formula that looked fairly foolproof. Because IBM's 360 series computers were obviously going to be the hottest thing on the market for a long time, resale values were safest if they concentrated on 360s. An occasional big computer from CDC or Univac nonetheless found its way onto a leasing company's list of assets, and several manufacturers spawned leasing companies of their own. The 360-based companies realized that they were totally dependent on IBM's continued maintenance. They were also completely vulnerable to the early introduction of a new generation of IBM computers. The 360 had been announced in April 1964. The magic date for the next generation could be 1970.

Maturing in its own brash way along with the computer industry, the leasing industry went on a wild buying spree in the late sixties, trying to turn some of its high turnover into something less comparable to Chinese paper money. Software companies were high on the shopping lists. So were bureaus and peripheral manufacturers. The leasing companies had to be in a position to evaluate whatever new developments came along, which meant that they had to have computer experts of their own so they might as well skim some of the profits that were coming into the services side of the computer industry. Business overseas was also beginning to boom. By 1968 there was an intense invasion into Britain, with bids and counterbids for software companies, parliamentary questions and impassioned leaders in the Sunday papers, culminating in London's great Leasco/Pergamon fuss.

THE LEASCO EXAMPLE

Leasco exemplifies some of the brightest thinking and the most severe problems of the computer leasing industry as a whole. Early into the business, Leasco was also one of the first to realize that it needed its own affiliation with a cash-generating institution. Leasco was one of the first to venture overseas, with a permanent organization and an offer to the Inbucon/AIC consulting and bureau group—an offer that was so high it could not be refused, raising a storm in the financial community that lasted many months. Disgruntled alumni still claim that Leaso offered four times the company's own valuation of its worth.

Leasco was one of the first to see that having its own chain of bureaus could be profitable, and could also provide lodging and remunerative work for middle-aged 360 systems as they were retired from their original leases. Leasco was one of the first to try for its own software and maintenance capabilities, not only for their commercial value but also to give a measure of insurance in case IBM should begin to view the leasing industry with a less friendly eye. Leasco was first to see that databases would be important in the seventies.

Leasco also saw the potential in the terminal business exceptionally early, and bought into U.S. and European companies before most of its competitors began shopping. Steinberg's strategic planning continued to be superb, and drew more and more attention as the computer and financial worlds waited breathlessly to find out what he'd do next.

The problems at Leasco were also characteristic of the computer industry as a whole and of the leasing industry, amplified somewhat by the glare of this public attention. The young financial wizards who had created the leasing business and kept it moving with their superb market antennae had very little experience in running other kinds of businesses such as banks, software houses, bureaus, consultancies, terminal companies—or foreign companies. My theory about the cause of the ensuing debacle is that they believed that people in these companies were motivated by the same entrepreneurial factors that kept their own fires burning.

Steinberg has referred to an "in, up, and out" personnel policy at Leasco. He maintains that his company has always moved people up quickly. Then if it found they could not do a job, it invited them to depart or demoted them, making room for other eager contenders. Journalist Hedley Voysey once quipped that the half-life of a Leasco vice-president was six months.

This approach to management was foreign to the financial institutions, and even more foreign when the leasing companies went overseas. Few of them realized with what shock and anger their host countries viewed the casual dehiring of eminent consultants or managers. Inbucon/AIC, for example, was not really assimilated into the Leasco organization (for this reason, I believe), and built up stony walls of silence between itself and its new parent.

Leasco's earliest software investments were similarly foreign—companies doing specialized business, much of it for the U.S. government. Lumping several of these together, dumping in new management, and then streamlining the result did not overnight increase their business or profitability. Quite the reverse. Software specialists are as rare as tropical fish, and require equally delicate and knowledgeable handling. Here and there, little groups began to depart, sometimes taking chunks of business with them.

The bureau ventures were similarly perilous. Financial wizardry, as many companies know to their sorrow, is no protection against software that is perennially 90 percent finished. Leasco was early into the time-sharing business, and seemed surprised to find that it took much more money and several more years to get established with a workable system than the plans had forecast. The true networks of bureaus in the United States and Europe that had been planned never materialized at all—a combination of telecommunications delays and R&D time passing until the funds were no longer so comfortably available.

On the financial side, Leasco received a severe blow in 1969 when a congressional committee exploring the computer leasing business growled that it would not look kindly upon any plans Leasco might have to invest $39 million in surplus surplus cash generated by its subsidiary Reliance Insurance Company into computer-related activities. That same summer, Leasco's attempt to take over Pergamon Press, with its warehouses full of technical information (all potential computer databases) had gone wildly and noisily awry, leaving Leasco with many millions tied up in Pergamon stock (whose value could not be determined for several years) but no control of the company. In the process, some Leasco/Pergamon plans to take over a major European source of technical databases also came to nought. Then in mid-1971 a Brooklyn court decided Leasco was liable for damages from irate Reliance stockholders. It said Leasco had neglected to mention $100 million in surplus surplus cash (beyond the legal requirement) in the 1968 prospectus offering Leasco shares to Reliance stockholders.

Meanwhile, back on Wall Street, computer fads were decidedly going out of fashion. If your name were Transworld Leasing, Time-Sharing and

Software Systems (the 1967 analogy to "Lincoln's Doctor's Dog" on the Wall Street best seller list), you could no longer get an underwriter to take you out to lunch. Stock prices began to fall in computer leasing, and with them fell the acquisition ability that had maintained much of the late-sixties momentum. IBM's 1969 unbundling announcement added its own uncertainties, though the giant company made it clear it would honor maintenance agreements for existing computers. (Most leases were written with direct maintenance contracts between IBM and the user.) But the leasing companies not only depended on these agreements for their equipment on lease to "third parties," they also had to depend on the continued grace and favor of IBM in transferring the agreements as equipment came back to the lessors and was once again leased or sold to yet other parties. Furthermore, there were beginning to be rumbles of a new IBM series of computers once unbundling was established. A more aggressive IBM could wipe out the leasing industry entirely too easily.

Data Processing Financial and General (DPF&G), one of the more aggressive leasing companies (then led by a lawyer), initiated an antitrust lawsuit against IBM after the unbundling decision. Some of the others set up a lessor's association. Though the Wall Street situation never returned to its previous pleasantness, there were quiet sighs of relief as DPF&G called off its lawsuit. IBM gently rewrote some of its contracts with DPF&G, easing some of the pressure from many millions in overdue payments. IBM also delayed its new series until June 1970, then came out with a 360-compatible range of computers that did not wipe out the residual value of the older models overnight. Finally, IBM let it be known that if the lessor's association wanted to sell 360 equipment in Eastern Europe, maintenance and support could probably be provided from IBM's well-staffed Vienna outpost. After RCA bowed out of the computer business in September 1971, it seemed more in IBM's interests to keep little industries like leasing alive, if not thriving.

Today, like the computer industry itself, the computer leasing companies seem to have lived through their wild adolescence, and maturity seems to have moderated some of their unrealistic optimisms. There are still signs that IBM may not choose to maintain computers that go to inconvenient places or run up ferocious downtime records. This leaves a still-alarming vulnerability because the lessors would then have to provide such service themselves or make other arrangements. For postunbundling equipment, most people leasing computers contract directly with IBM for this support, and the sum is deducted from their leasing contract payments. This approach has relieved some of the pressure.

SHOULD YOU LEASE A COMPUTER?

With all the chaos of the leasing industry's childhood and adolescence, it is very easy to overlook the basic premise of computer leasing. It saved the user about 25 percent a month compared with the cost of leasing from the manufacturer. This gap has been gently narrowed by IBM since it announced its unbundling policies, but 10 to 15 percent is common still.

Every penny you don't spend on computer rental goes straight below the line, contributing to profit. I don't think any company can afford to ignore this kind of situation.

There are problems. Most leasing companies are now highly selective about the kinds of leases they want. They don't have the unlimited funds of the earlier decade, so they aren't likely to be very interested unless you're getting a 360 or 370 system in a fairly standard configuration. If there is a lot of systems work or special gear, it may require separate financing, though a few like Leasco can handle systems contracts from a manpower as well as a financial angle.

Some manufacturers now have their own leasing companies. Some peripheral makers and terminal companies have also made arrangements for the lease of their equipment, using fairly conservative write-off periods.

In all of these transactions, your contracts man is your first line of defense. The maintenance provisions are particularly tricky, and three-way discussions between your company, the lessor, and the computer manufacturer should take place before you sign any standard contracts.

If you are getting a system that you expect to keep forever, working around the clock, you may be better off buying it. The best way to evaluate the alternatives is probably a simple discounted cash flow calculation (which can be done on a time-sharing terminal if your accountant doesn't want to take the time himself). Some computer contracts still call for extra charges when a system works more than a specified number of hours.

Check into the range of services available for your system from the leasing company. Lessors have over $2,000,000,000 invested in computers in the United States alone—a large investment to protect. Many have made major investments in software to give new value to older computers. Packages and software assistance may be available for your system at reasonable cost from the lessor. The leasing company can also act as a clearing house for peripherals. Before you buy a new card reader, it's probably worth checking to see whether your friendly neighborhood lessor has a good reconditioned model lying around for lease or purchase.

Even though it is a little harder now to find a willing lessor and negotiate optimum terms, you are still the treasured customer deciding whether or not his services are what you want. Stay in the driver's seat.

9

Farming Out the Headaches

You can lease anything, from a motorcycle to a ten-ton truck. If you contract not only for your computing vehicle but for the operators, the service people, even the programmers and analysts—a part-time or full-time chauffeur-driven service—that's facilities management.

You can also buy specialized vehicles—campers, rolling demonstration buses, delivery vans—that are analogous to turnkey systems.

A great deal of confusion seems to have arisen between these two in particular, but the difference is simple. In facilities management (FM), the FM company takes over your computer or provides you with the use of one of theirs. In turnkey, you contract with a specialized company to build a system and turn it over to you ready to plug in (turn on the key) and run.

Another confusing term is the "systems contract," in which you farm out the total responsibility for a complete application or system. This more often applies to unique or very large systems, while turnkey contracts tend to be smaller—often in the computer-instrument class.

Two other kinds of service—the dedicated bureau and the subscription service—are sometimes confused with facilities management. Yet other permutations will develop as entrepreneurs go into the lucrative business of relieving computer-related headaches.

Each of these is very convenient in its proper place. All these types of contracts have the advantage that the user company can, to a large extent, concentrate its management resources on its primary business rather than diversifying against its better judgment into the computer business.

THE SYSTEMS CONTRACT

The systems contract originated in the United States when the air force and other armed forces found that they did not have enough experts to oversee the development of large missile or aerospace systems. Independent companies were found (or sometimes established for the purpose) to watch over major development projects and act as technical directors to other contractors while they simultaneously served as technical advisors to the end user. Hughes was one of the original systems companies, and progenitor to many in the aerospace field. Ramo-Wooldridge spun off first; then Space Technology Laboratories (STL, now Thompson-Ramo-Wooldridge Systems) separated itself from Ramo-Wooldridge. Finally the nonprofit Aerospace Corporation was formed when STL decided to go into the hardware business. Other nonprofits that depended on systems contracts from the air force included RAND, System Development Corp. (computing daughter of RAND), and Mitre, an MIT spin-off. One of the first computer-oriented systems companies was the Auerbach Corporation. Such aircraft companies as Lockheed, General Dynamics, Boeing, Martin-Marietta, and McDonnell (later McDonnell-Douglas) also found their way into lucrative SE/TD (Systems Engineering/Technical Direction) contracts until there was a profusion of nonprofit companies overseeing aerospace companies who were themselves overseeing hordes of subcontractors.

In the regular business world the systems contract is fortunately a simpler (and less expensive) phenomenon. It is nonetheless undertaken for the same purpose: to farm out to a company that is expert in computing much of the technical work and supervision that are needed for successful development of a complicated system.

It is impossible (and unwise to try) to farm out all of the evaluation and specification. It is also unwise to ignore the whole thing until it is done. The main advantage in a systems contract is that a reputable firm with special skills will accept responsibility for the usefulness of the resulting system.

Selection of a systems company requires even more care (and trust) than selection of a consulting company or software house, though the same firms may be under consideration. If your systems contractor were to go bankrupt part way through the task, you could be liable for more than the cost of completing some key programs—you could also find yourself forced to pay for a computer you thought was covered by your progress payments.

In addition to bankruptcy, you have to worry a little extra about the specification. An even more elaborate sequence of review meetings, written assignments, and written reports than that required for in-house feasibility studies is called for during the earliest phases.

Working closely with his client, the systems contractor develops detailed specifications, evaluates equipment, contracts for the computer mainframe and peripheral equipment, designs special devices or interfaces as they are needed, writes or oversees the writing of programs, evaluates packaged programs on occasion, and makes sure the documentation of the hardware, software, and operating procedures is adequate. He also trains your people to use the system; this is most effective if your user department people, in addition to your computer department people, are given sufficient training. Finally, he turns over a workable—and working—system.

Systems contracts can and should have clear definitions of when the resulting system is deemed to have passed its acceptance tests. They should also carry penalties for delay. If the systems contractor is unwilling to stand behind his work by accepting a penalty claim, find out why. You may have created an impossible specification. But without this kind of guarantee, you aren't getting the peace of mind you're paying for in a systems contract.

Phaseless contracts are another danger. The systems contract is particularly well suited to large systems, with some measure of development work involved. If you contract separately first for the feasibility and specification phases, you will have a clearer idea of how the contractor works and how well you suit each other by the time you reach the evaluation and development phases.

It may be wise to have an independent consultant (one you know and trust) sit in on the review meetings. But few companies can afford the tiers of over-overseers that characterized the early systems contracts for the U.S. Air Force. If you do choose to have this kind of watchdog, make sure you don't get bogged down in small technical differences between the two.

TURNKEY SYSTEMS

While the systems contract is suited to large systems with some development content, the turnkey contract is more often for a smaller, specialized system. There are turnkey companies that specialize in such applications as process control, telecommunications, or personnel records.

Shop-floor applications not only tend to have a rather high payoff, they also lend themselves well to turnkey contracting. A rather small computer can handle process plant control, for example, more cheaply and reliably than it can be handled by some of the special equipment based on relay logic that is usually used in industry. Automatic logging systems are now working effectively in many monitoring applications, often with special alarms and printouts whenever certain operations or values go outside normal limits. These systems can handle hundreds of inputs from digital counters or analog readouts that have been fed in through analog-to-digital converters. Because they are programmable (their software can be changed), such computers can also accommodate the changes in procedure or instrumentation that were often impossible with special-purpose, hard-wired systems.

Automatic warehousing can be controlled by a small computer. According to one expert,[1] high-bay warehouses operated with stacker cranes can be fully or partially controlled by turnkey systems, as can the transport of goods to and from the cranes. Most systems provide manual override or intervention to assure users that they, and not the computers, are actually running the system. The multilevel warehouse has a trolley for each level, handling goods on pallets as they come from an input bay, stacking them in roller conveyor lanes, from which they can be fetched for delivery to output bays. These systems are harder to operate manually, so two computers are often used to give proper backup. Both can feed stock control information back to a central system.

In addition to controlling events in a factory environment, the turnkey system can often be programmed to do some analyzing and optimizing. If you are dealing with a turnkey company that specializes in shop-floor applications, you can be sure that most potentially fruitful frills and decorations for the system will be proposed during the course of negotiations. The "start slow" proviso for new applications may be particularly important for shop-floor systems, where many people may be affected. Nonetheless, make sure that your configuration does not lock you out of future uses that might have high payoff.

Selection of a turnkey company is often a much simpler matter than the choice of a software house or systems contractor, though many companies with general computer competence will happily volunteer to do

1. "On Line for Quick Thinking," *The Engineer,* June 30, 1971, London, England.

jobs on a turnkey basis. If specialist companies of similar standing are available (though they may be smaller and younger), you may find the job costs less or the system does slightly more. In this instance, references from previous clients should be particularly relevant to your own task.

In most turnkey systems, a rather small computer is dedicated to a single task. Once the specifications have been reviewed and settled and you are confident that the turnkey company understands the unique procedures in your own company that affect the system, overseeing the progress need not be very time-consuming. Again, the company should be willing to accept penalty clauses. Remember that changes will cost an inordinate sum once you have given the go-ahead.

You are delegating a great deal of the technical work in a turnkey contract, but you must still define your acceptance test standards. You should also be responsible for furnishing proper test data (both sample batches and worst-case artificial data), in addition to any other data the contractor needs to design the system. It will have to be based on your own file structures unless it works completely independently from any other systems in your company. Acceptance testing should be included in the delivery date agreement. The contractor should also be willing to give you a warranty period, during which he promises to correct any defects that show up after delivery. Though there are computer programs whose bugs don't show up for several years, it would be unreasonable to hold a turnkey company to this kind of warranty period; he would be sensible to charge you more if you insisted on this kind of ongoing overseeing.

Logica, Ltd., a turnkey company that is particularly known for its telecommunications systems, points out that many contracts are written on a time-and-materials basis (rather than a fixed-price basis) with fixed prices for the hardware. Logica notes that the hardware can be paid for at any time during the development period, but higher interest rates are charged if payment is very close to the completion date. Monthly progress payments are common.

If the turnkey contractor raises his charges or makes any other major changes part way through a contract, you should retain the right to terminate the contract, with the circumstances and settlements clearly spelled out. In the event of a dispute (less likely than in other kinds of computer contracts), your local computer society can often furnish an arbitrator.

The turnkey contractor will probably specify that the programs and the system he has furnished you are proprietary and should not be given to other companies. Similarly, he should treat as confidential any corporate information he requires from you for proper completion of the system.

FACILITIES MANAGEMENT

Facilities management can come into your company at the beginning of a computer project or much later. In either case, the facilities manager takes some or all of your computing worries off your shoulders—for a fee. In essence, it becomes your data processing department. Not only will the facilities management company buy your computer (if you own it) or take over the lease, it will also take over your people in most contracts.

A Texan named Ross Perot has been called Saul Steinberg's counterpart in the facilities management business. The former IBM salesman realized that a number of companies would pay most happily to delegate all of their computing problems to an outside company if they could go on having the same level of service or improved service on their own premises. Perot founded a company called Electronic Data Systems (EDS) that took off like a rocket in facilities management, and on Wall Street, although a sharp drop during the 1970 recession cut Perot's personal net worth by more than $140 million in a single day.

Financial fads notwithstanding, the facilities management idea is growing rapidly, particularly among larger American companies. It is equally (sometimes better) suited to medium-sized companies or smaller ones with a relatively high computing workload but insufficient resources to afford the specialists it needs.

An underutilized computer or widely varying demand make facilities management particularly attractive. According to the Hoskyns Group, which has begun to undertake FM contracts in Britain, companies spending up to $250,000 annually on their computing are the most likely prospects for facilities management.

Figure 9-1 shows my interpretation of the annual savings calculated by *Computer Management* magazine[2] for facilities management in various usage situations. It can be seen immediately that the closer you get to steady two-shift or three-shift usage, the more the benefits shift toward

2. "Delegation, Not Abdication," *Computer Management,* June 1971, London, England.

in-house computers. FM and in-house costs were equal for one-shift running.

Although it may charge you what you are already spending for one-shift operation, a facilities management firm can afford the experts to give the installation an extremely thorough audit, tune it up with sharp operations procedures, and skim off surplus people. The facilities manager then finds himself with a little extra time to sell or a few spare people. Like the computer time, they are often deployed elsewhere at a profit.

In the American style, facilities management contracts carried certain perils for the computer workers in user companies, and tended on occasion to stir up fear and dissension. The staff automatically became employees of the FM company overnight, and had no assurance that they

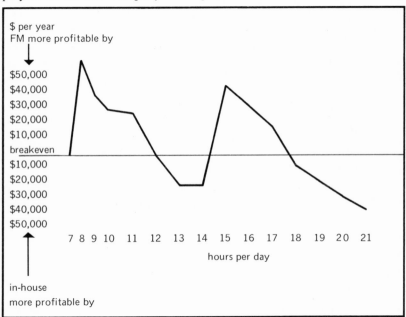

Assumptions:

Seven hours per shift available for operation, one hour for maintenance.

A regular number of hours per day required. Where the requirement per day fluctuates, FM will show greater savings.

A minimum of one shift was the FM requirement in this case. FM and in-house costs were equal for one shift.

Fig. 9-1. Breakeven points for facilities management.

would be retained in the same installation. For many competent operators, programmers, and analysts, the challenge of working in a more professional environment was exhilarating, and better work resulted. Others, unable or unwilling to cope with the insecurity, found work elsewhere, so most staff reductions took place by attrition.

Many companies, particularly larger ones, have chosen to separate the functions, retaining their own systems analysts and programmers, but farming out the computing itself. The systems staff (even in a smaller company) can then specify and oversee any enhancements to the hardware or software that the facilities management company makes to meet the user's needs. This seems a sensible separation, and will probably become more common as more computers are run under facilities management contracts. Whether there is an in-house systems group or not, the user should keep sufficient capability to oversee systems development on the same phased basis that it would be carried out in-house. The new developments are normally charged for by the FM company on the same scale as for any other software house or consulting company. It is wise to keep in mind that when you select a facilities manager, you are also selecting your future systems contractor, software house, and consultant in one decision, for a period that probably lasts at least five years. Operational efficiency requires one kind of skill. Particularly if you are in an expansion phase with respect to computing, make sure the other kinds of skills are also likely to be present when you need them.

When the facilities manager takes over your computer, he also takes over your programs. Unless yours is an exceptional installation, some of these will be less than perfect, poorly documented, awkward, but useful nonetheless. The ownership of these programs, particularly any that you think might have commercial value, should be clearly specified in the contract. If they remain your property, you may have to pay for upgrading or maintenance at either a fixed annual rate or standard programming rates for the time required, just as you would have had to pay for your own people to maintain or upgrade them. The facilities manager may be able to develop new programs for you or amend packages at rates somewhat more favorable than your own small group could have achieved. Again, make sure ownership of the new programs is taken into account when fees are negotiated.

The method of payment for facilities management differs from one facilities manager to another, and even from one client to another. There is always room for negotiation. Hoskyns charges on several different bases for computer time: an hourly charge (based on only the productive hours, not the start-up or maintenance or other overhead functions); or a price per transaction (such as a payslip). In either system, the contract should specify whether the contractor or the client supplies the forms, tapes, disks, and other materials that are used.

Data preparation is normally charged on a per-card or a per-record basis, comparable to a data preparation bureau. There may be extra charges when balancing, sorting, or other forms of work on unit records takes an appreciable amount of time. The charges may also vary according to the quality of the inputs—as indeed they should in any installation.

THE DEDICATED BUREAU

The dividing line between facilities management and a dedicated bureau is very fine indeed. This is often a facility that has been sufficiently centralized to operate as an in-house bureau, with its own expert staff. Whether it is a wholly owned subsidiary, owned by another company entirely, or a joint venture, it usually operates its prime shift for a single company, then runs for other companies or another parent in the remaining shifts. The same contractual choices exist, and like the facilities management company, the dedicated bureau needs a long-term commitment to do its own corporate planning. Thus three- to five-year contracts are common.

When a dedicated bureau is owned by an external body, the client company has an enormous life-and-death power over the bureau's destiny (and vice versa), so the bureau must protect itself with a contract that spells out who is to be responsible for an enormous list of possible disasters. Expansion is again an important factor; the ability to run a dedicated bureau does not insure that a firm has systems contracting ability. Ownership of mutually developed programs is also a problem that must be contractually resolved, sometimes on a program-by-program basis.

The in-house computer department that is run on a bureau basis for its clients in various other departments of the corporation can often operate more successfully than one that makes no visible charges for its services. The decision as to how to price services is a delicate one. The in-house bureau should be seen to operate on the same profit-and-loss accountability basis as other elements of the company. On the other hand, if this forces its charges to be too high (so profits are high), the captive clients may get restive, especially if comparable services are available from commercial bureaus at lower rates. An in-house bureau that runs consistently but modestly in the black, carries on any necessary system development competently, and charges less than outside services would charge is obviously the optimum. The temptation for such bureaus to sell their spare time outside is almost irresistible when they operate on a strict profit-and-loss basis. The hazards of in-house/out-house bureaus are discussed in greater detail in Chapter 11.

THE SUBSCRIPTION SERVICE

Combining some of the merits of facilities management, specialized turnkey contracting, and the dedicated bureau is the subscription service —a relatively new phenomenon in the computer services spectrum. These companies blur very easily into specialized bureaus—the only official distinction may be that they were created by the combined efforts of a small group of users and continue to serve that group, rather than offering their services more widely.

If you have a major application that calls for a special configuration and considerable investment in development, but will not eventually require the full resources of the computer around the clock, it may be worthwhile looking for other companies with similar needs. Such cooperative developments can often be carried out independently by facilities management type companies or systems contractors, then run either by the FM people or by a joint venture group set up for the purpose. Several bureaus that specialize in construction industry applications, for example, were founded in this manner.

If you are setting up a subscription service on a joint venture basis, the services of a first-class contracts man will pay off handsomely. The relationships between the various clients and the service company can be delicate when the clients are competitors in the same industry.

A weary accountant once commented that a business partnership involved more trust and interdependence than a marriage. Both suffer whenever there is an inability to choose partners wisely or spell out the relationships clearly. In a joint venture, the scheduling and priorities will cause problems unless these policies are clearly defined at the beginning. Even the location of the bureau can be contentious, especially if it is doing batch work, where pickup and delivery responsibilities and schedules must be worked out. In remote batch work, the presence of a local terminal can ease some of the natural worries that the competitor/partners are getting better service.

GETTING YOUR MONEY'S WORTH

All of these services offer relief from detailed computer worries. They can, and often do, keep a company's top management concentrating on strategies in its own business, while competent computer people provide the necessary tools to operate competitively.

The make-or-buy decisions for these services must take into account one vital distinction: are you avoiding an unwanted diversification into the computer business, or farming out a function that is fundamental to your company's operations? In either case, this calls for some decision as to the level of systems analysis capability you choose to keep inside the user departments of the company as a whole.

Once you have decided to farm out anything from systems development to special applications to the day-to-day running of the computer, two guidelines will keep you out of the majority of troubles:

1. Make sure that expansion needs have been taken into consideration before you enter into long-term commitments to a company or into a configuration.
2. Use the best contracts man you can find, to make sure that interrelationships and responsibilities are spelled out clearly.

Computer Management carried a number of other useful articles on these aspects of the services industry during 1971. A précis of the turnkey and facilities management phenomena also appeared in the computer survey article in *The Economist* on February 16, 1971.

10

Buying Secondhand Computers

"Perfect condition," says the used-car salesman. "It was just used by a little old lady from Camden Town to drive to church on Sundays." His prospective customer may be a young man looking for his first car, a commuter who needs an inexpensive model to leave at the station every morning, or a family that wants something big enough to handle the children and the groceries.

A secondhand computer may be an equally sensible investment. In fact, it is slightly more likely to keep on running satisfactorily than the secondhand car. The little old lady may have been a rally driver, or forgetful when it came to changing the oil. The first user of the computer, on the other hand, was probably backed up with first-class maintenance from the manufacturer.

Price is your chief benefit in choosing a secondhand computer. Owing to rapid change and business uncertainties, late models are often available. It has been estimated that a computer system that cost $1 million to purchase and install in 1969 will be available for under $100,000 by the mid-seventies.

WHEN TO USE THEM

Whenever your company seems to be outgrowing its computer facilities, there are a number of alternatives to consider. An audit may help you defer expansion for a year or two. Bureaus are getting better, and may take overflow loads off your present computer, or even handle new applications. You can hire a facilities management company to take over the whole thing, or bring in a software house to optimize some of your programs.

If your present computer is of a fairly ordinary variety and has been working fairly satisfactorily with its existing programs (which is often the case with second-generation computers whose programs have had a few years of seasoning), an identical used computer may be particularly attractive. The two can normally occupy your present facilities ("back-to-back" in computer terminology). Then it may not be necessary to duplicate all peripherals. Furthermore, you can get the manufacturer or a hardware consultant to create a cross-switching mechanism, even a memory-sharing device that allows one computer to operate if the other is out of order or being maintained. The more "real" you demand your response time to be, the more this type of arrangement is likely to cost.

If you are already using a machine in the IBM 1401 or 1130 class, this type of backup has another advantage. It is now possible to buy relatively inexpensive conversion kits that include the hardware and software (plus installation and sometimes some training and documentation) that allow you to change one of your twin systems to a time-sharing system, usually for eight simultaneous in-house users. This means that for the cost of a used computer (normally less than half a new one) you can have internal time sharing plus several shifts of additional batch processing, without the expense of changing all your programs.

Even for first-time users who are bargain hunting, the used computer offers certain advantages; 360-class computers, especially the earlier models, are readily available at attractive prices (often with full maintenance from the manufacturer), well dressed in workable programs.

Programs tend to age well, like good brandy; the older they get, the better they are. Mundane, businesslike programs for these machines are likely to be almost bug-free. Programmers to amend them or write new ones are also less expensive than the latest models, though the harm done by a mediocre programmer can offset any savings in labor costs. Documentation, on the other hand, may be rudimentary if you are getting your machine from another user or hiring older-generation programmers. There is a sufficient choice available of both machines and programmers so that you can insist on adequate documentation with the machine and in your programs under development. The specification or contract is the key instrument in this respect.

Once in a while the computer makers suffer the same fate as the car makers: they turn out a lemon. I don't mean the generic lemon, like the Edsel that could never live up to its market research; I mean the specific lemon, which arrives with a bad starter motor, breaks a fan belt every week, has a constitutional grunch in the differential gear, and chronic carburetor trouble. Fortunately, lemons are less common in the computer mainframe business than in the car business, but they happen. (Secondhand peripherals carry more risk of this nature.) If you *do* happen to get one, identify it as quickly as possible, then encourage the manufacturer to trade straight across for an identical model that works. If the local people are not enthusiastic at this prospect, you might paint lemons on it, take some snapshots, and send them to the company's vice-president in charge of public relations. This worked very well with automobiles in the fifties, so there's no reason to abandon the technique in the seventies.

Like handing down the old Volkswagen to your wife or son when you decide to buy a new Ford, you may provide your own secondhand computer to an outlying facility. If it is a workable system whose quirks are known, transferring it with several knowledgeable caretakers makes sense if you are trading up. Its value to you is probably far higher than its trade-in value would be to the manufacturer or to another user. The known quirks, the known programs, and the availability of known people to help during the changeover can make a major difference. If the new machine can use the old one as a remote terminal, you are well on your way to an internal network. Judicious addition of other computers of the same ilk (preferably one at a time) could give you a centralized network at relatively low cost in money or internal chaos.

The administrative and technical problems are generally less when a secondhand computer is added than when you trade up to the latest technology. Multiprogramming, for example, requires very different approaches to control, programming, scheduling, and operation. It can also save a great deal of money when it is used properly. Most companies are catapulted into multiprogramming when someone sells them large new computers, adding the major technical challenges of a complete new technique to the already oversized organizational problem of assimilating any new computer. A twin for Old Faithful seldom stirs up the organization, and new techniques (including multiprogramming and time sharing) can be added at your leisure. They may not run as fast on Old Faithful, but it often saves money to be able to iron out the problems in an orderly fashion, rather than to create new ones in real time. When the new techniques are working well enough to reveal how old and slow Old Faithful really is, he can be given honorable retirement to a quiet subsidiary or traded in for a new model.

WHERE TO BUY THEM

As computers are losing some of their glamour, the number of sources for secondhand computers is growing rapidly. Thus, "blue book" buy-and-sell rates are available on many standard models from companies that specialize in computer resale.

Because the majority of their products are out on lease, and therefore return to the fold when users trade up, the manufacturers themselves are one of the better sources of secondhand computers. Control Data Corporation has set up a separate organization to handle secondhand sales. Others are quite willing to furnish lists of available configurations, though these are unlikely to be forthcoming from your friendly neighborhood computer salesman until he is convinced that you will not be buying one of his new models.

Even used peripherals such as IBM's model 2314 disk system can be purchased direct from the manufacturers. These will normally be reconditioned by the maker to work as well as they did when they were new. Peripherals have more electromechanical parts that are subject to wear than mainframes have—mainframes, like programs, tend to improve with age. First-generation computers, based on unreliable vacuum tubes, are usually sold for scrap or collectors' pieces; there is virtually no other market for them. Some early-generation business machines like the Royal-McBee LGP-30, which were and are useful equipment, are sufficiently archaic to be available now and then for absurdly low prices (several thousand dollars at most). If you have use for such machines (and an LGP-30 lover willing to look after the old dears—they engendered close emotional ties in their first users), they may be worth the cost to move them to your facilities.

Much more to the point are the second- and early third-generation computers that can go on being useful as adjuncts to next-generation networks.

According to the Boston Computer Group, Inc., more than $10 billion worth of computer hardware is heading eventually for the used computer market—about 30 percent of the estimated $35 billion worth of computers installed in the United States in 1970. U.S. secondhand computer sales in 1970 were about $50 million—a small percentage of the total potential supply, but double the 1969 quantity. The computer manufacturers will continue to handle a healthy portion of this growing business.

So will the leasing companies, who owned about $2,800,000,000 worth of IBM equipment in 1970, and about $700 million more from other manufacturers. They have a strong pressure to sell some of these systems as they come back off lease because they need the money to invest in new computer leases. The maintenance agreements may be somewhat less straightforward if you are getting your secondhand machine from a leasing company than if you deal with a manufacturer. Programs may not be as forthcoming as they would from the manufacturer's library either, but the costs tend to be a trifle less.

Other users are also a major source of secondhand computers. Very suitable machines can sometimes be found through trade associations or individual inquiries, but a much more common source of computers from other users is the secondhand computer broker, a new breed but clearly a buoyant one. The broker usually takes his commission just like a used-car dealer, from the top. Small classified advertisements in the computer press can sometimes save the cost of this commission, though a good broker (like a good used-car salesman) will have certain warranty and mainte- nance services that make the more standard transaction attractive.

When you are buying a used computer from another end user, there is usually a lot of room for negotiation. He would rather sell it to you as long as he can get more than the computer manufacturer is willing to offer for a trade-in. But you may not want his programs for payroll, accounting, stock control, or anything else, particularly if you are just looking for a twin to share Old Faithful's already capable software. It's still worth the time to look over the list if programs are being offered as an enticement to buy.

HOW TO BUY THEM

Parke-Bernet Galleries, a New York affiliate of Sotheby's, held an auction of used computer equipment in 1970 that ranged from a museum- piece Univac I console (sold as a wall decoration for a few hundred dol- lars) to some very useful 360/20 systems. Most of the equipment was sold for prices that pleased the gallery and the original owners, yet pro- vided bargain hunters with a pleasant day out.

It is doubtful that many art galleries will take up computer auctions as a sideline. Auctions will dwindle as more used gear comes on the market, while the prices will become more firmly established.

By 1971 fairly clear prices were available for many popular second-hand machines. Second-generation machines in general cost about 25 percent of their original value. A classic IBM 1401, which cost from $170,000 to $350,000 when it was new in the early sixties, could usually be purchased for about $30,000 to $100,000 in the United States, though prices in Britain tended to be a bit higher—the 1401 was not such a best seller in the United Kingdom, so supplies are more limited. The percentages overlook one additional benefit: the cost of debugging a new computer and its programs. The $350,000 system may have cost its user $500,000 or more before he had it running properly.

The third-generation 360/20 is probably the hottest item in the used-computer market. It accounted for the greatest number of IBM installations in its prime, and is beautifully suited to use as a remote batch terminal, connected to a larger 360 or 370 computer. Prices for the 360/20 are expected to hold fairly firmly at about 50 percent of the original price, and can sometimes run as high as 75 percent for late models with considerable communications gear.

The slightly larger 360/30 (which was IBM's favored replacement for the trusty 1401) is also holding around the 50 percent level, though top prices seldom go above 70 percent of original cost. These resale values are not likely to drop too sharply for the next few years.

Secondhand equipment from other manufacturers is not likely to cost quite so much, though the selection may not be so large. The manufacturer will often provide a great deal of assistance in finding other end users who want to sell if you can't find anything in their secondhand showrooms to suit you. Some fairly new non-IBM systems, like Honeywell's smaller computers in the 16 series, are available generally for 30 percent or less of the original cost.

Both the manufacturers and leasing companies have residual values to support—the old computers they own are assets on their financial statements. Therefore, even if the supply of computers available for resale goes up much more rapidly than the demand, the two largest sources are unlikely to react with price cuts below a certain level. Nonetheless, secondhand computers are likely to remain a buyer's market, so you are in a position to demand first-class extras.

A warranty, for instance, can give you the same protection you get with a new computer, though it may give you a shorter period in which to uncover defects.

Unless you are purchasing an obsolete and ancient oddity, you can expect and negotiate for full support for operating systems and applications programs. Older machines are also well furnished with user groups that have useful libraries of programs. If you imply that you are interested in applications programs, you will have an enormous list of programs, all free and fully documented, dangled before your dazzled eyes. Disregard the length of the list (many items on it are N-Dimensional routines for Widget engineers), nod sagely, and pass copies to your user departments. You may find unexpected treasures in the castoffs jumbled around in secondhand computer stores.

11

Using Service Bureaus

Why tie up capital in a fleet of cars when you can hire limousines or taxis instead? Your own car entails fixed costs for insurance, depreciation, and taxes, whether you drive it 10 miles or 100,000 miles a year. If you need it to travel regularly between places that are otherwise inconvenient or hard to reach, the expense is probably justified. If you live a short bus ride from your office and work regular hours, the car is probably a luxury. Many companies lease fleets of cars, retain taxi services, and regularly pay air fares and train tickets to make sure that their people get where they need to go by the most suitable means.

Why buy a computer (not to mention the expensive computer room, air conditioning, specialist staff, and organizational chaos) when you can use a computer bureau instead? Why buy a cow when milk is so cheap?

There are often good reasons for having your own computer, just as there are for having your own car. Control of schedules and priorities can be important. Costs are sometimes less if you know your own needs. It may be essential for some part of the company and convenient for others. But many of these factors were more valid five years ago than they are now.

As the entire spectrum of computer services comes into its own, the service bureaus are growing particularly rapidly. Two factors have accelerated this growth: IBM's 1969 unbundling announcement, and the economic slumps that hit the United States in 1969-70 and Europe in 1971. In the United Kingdom the situation was intensified by a simultaneous change in government attitudes toward bureau use for its own departments and by a change in its investment grant policy that had an immediate effect on cash flow. Instead of cash reimbursement to companies investing in computers, the government gave generous tax credits.

In this new atmosphere, users began to defer new computer purchases on both sides of the Atlantic. As the level of business dropped slightly, users began to look at their fixed overheads. Computers were one of these, but were often coming under scrutiny for the first time. Those companies with underutilized computers began to see their relatively fixed computing costs shoot up astronomically as a percentage of overall costs. It has been estimated that even a medium-sized magnetic tape installation costs about $20,000 per month to run.

A number of companies reevaluated these costs, looked at their computer applications, and began shifting some or all of their work to bureaus. Even where the bureau services were slightly more expensive on a per-transaction basis than in-house systems, the users were able to pay only for those services they needed. They didn't have to pay for downtime that was due to power strikes, reruns, or bugs in the software. Thus they were reducing not only the actual outlay but also the risk.

The change affected the attitudes of computer people, too. Instead of finding a "virgin" company and building up a huge computer empire inside it, the DP manager who wanted to make his mark began to look for an overpopulated computer room where he could send back some of the machines, shift some of the staff out to user departments, and cut costs to the bone. Most computer departments could cut their hardware and staff by 50 percent without suffering much degradation in service. However, this can only be accomplished when both the company and the DP man have shifted their sights, so the decision to use whatever service is most cost effective becomes a routine part of the DP management function.

The shift from internal computing to service bureaus may be self-perpetuating. As their order books grew more slender during the recessions, the computer manufacturers were forced to lay people off and cut back on recruitment and training. Some of the brightest graduates in computer science and mathematics in 1970 and 1971 found their jobs with users and bureaus. They in turn will help attract more bright graduates. The immediate effect may be negligible, but these people will probably swing the pendulum still further toward the computer user. This seems to be another indication of a more basic trend. The sophisticated user is where the action is for computer people today. The manufacturers no longer offer a challenge to the majority of good programmers the way they did in the fifties and early sixties. Among the most sophisticated and professional users, one must count the computer service bureaus.

BUREAU CREDIBILITY

Undercapitalized, overoptimistic bureaus with technological stars in their eyes were among the first to go when hard times set in in the computer industry. But in the same environment, as more companies used outside services with some degree of satisfaction, the more businesslike bureaus found they were working in an atmosphere of increased acceptance and credibility.

Once their feet were wet, most users found a number of reasons to continue using bureaus. All of the reasons boil down to lower costs, effective service, and specialized capabilities that would be difficult or impossible to develop in-house.

Computers and programmers are the bureau's primary resources. One important difference between an industrial user and a service bureau is that a lack of good planning and control can cause difficulties for the user, but they cause a bureau to go broke. Conversely, the company that specializes in providing computer services can afford to put a larger percentage of its money into computer hardware. Thus, the user need not diversify into a technology that is unrelated to his business, but can still have the use of the latest and best computers.

Similarly, many bright programmers and analysts tend to become bored with the tasks they are assigned or frustrated by the lack of professional challenge and associates inside a smaller company. They also prefer the slightly higher pay scales that are traditionally found in bureaus. Managing such people effectively is also a special skill, critical to the success of a system but foreign to many traditional companies. Thus, as these programmers and managers gravitated toward each other in the more professionally challenging bureaus and software houses, the programs written there improved in quality. Today, bureau programs tend to run efficiently. Professional project management means they're usually tailored to the bureau's own hardware configuration, and they can also be tailored to the user's application, particularly if it is a large one.

If you are having a bureau package tailored or a new application written for you by bureau people, make sure your own people participate fully in the development. Not only will they understand the resulting program better, but the bureau people will understand the company and the application better.

The growing concern over privacy and the security of computerized information has also given a boost to bureaus. Bureau systems have to be more security conscious than in-house systems. Just as banks must take care not only to protect other people's money, but also to be *seen* to be protecting it, so bureaus must take extra precautions to make sure data is not lost, tapes and disk-packs are treated properly, unauthorized remote users do not get access to a client's business information, and outsiders are not permitted in the bureau's inner sanctum.

Another advantage of using a bureau is that it tends to build-in controls at its own end of the system. This cannot help but encourage the user to build-in controls at his own end. In other words, the bureau imposes a discipline that is often lacking in in-house systems.

It all sounds very reasonable and rosy. The arguments for computer service bureaus are indeed persuasive. However, there are flaws, even in this best of all possible worlds. A classic horror story concerns the British bureau that decided to rewrite its payroll programs in time for decimalization day in early 1971. A bug in the most important program caused every client's history for the year to go up in smoke—six weeks before the end of the tax year. Even though this is an almost apocryphal example, it would be sensible to look at the various types of bureaus that offer computer services and consider their pitfalls as well as their benefits. Bureaus can be sorted according to their computers, their applications specialties, or a number of other ways. I prefer to lump them into five (often overlapping) categories that reflect basic "personality differences":

- in-house/out-house bureaus
- time-sharing bureaus
- computer utilities
- specialized bureaus
- classic batch bureaus

Each has its own place in the business environment. Before exploring these separate categories, the broader subject of remote computing deserves some exploration.

THE JARGON

The trend toward remote computing is having a profound effect on computer make-or-buy decisions. All the new computers are designed to accommodate remote users. Terminals of all shapes and sizes are advertised like soap flakes in the technical press, at prices that are still dropping and will continue to do so until they reach a sensible equilibrium. Telephone facilities for teleprocessing are still a major hurdle. So is the proliferation of jargon.

It is impossible to count the claimants for the world's first "on-line," "real-time," "real-time on-line conversational," "remote-job-entry," "time-sharing," "remote-batch," or "three-dimensional" systems. There are user definitions and manufacturer definitions that differ widely for the same terms. In some cases (such as "real time") there are as many definitions as there are people who use the term. A manager simply needs to be able to cut through the foliage to know what he's getting. For purposes of this book, here are my own stripped-down definitions:

> *Teleprocessing* itself is a very simple and elegant concept. If data can be sent over telephone lines, it shouldn't matter to the user where his computer is located, or how many other people are using it.

"If" is the crux of the matter. Much of today's teleprocessing takes place over normal telephone circuits, the same networks that carry voice conversations from one location to another, anywhere in the world. These networks are getting cluttered with voices and data faster than the telephone companies can justify the huge expenditures they must make to add new facilities. There are special networks in development for data transmission, but until they are up and running and debugged, this will continue to be a problem. Thus it is wise to give as much advance notice as possible to the phone company when you expect to be doing teleprocessing. Large users who can justify the expense often lease private telephone lines for their data, just as they do for heavy intracompany volumes of voice conversations. These lines, too, are in critically short supply.

> *Real time* simply means returning results fast enough to do something about them.

"Real time" to the computer manufacturer actually means a transaction-oriented system. This affects the entire philosophy of control software and priority interrupts in the hardware, which must as a result push the microsecond and nanosecond barriers. To the user, a "real-time" system must be able to furnish the information he needs, when he needs it, reflecting the real situation at that time. (Often he needs on-time more than he needs real time.) This discrepancy explains in part why the user is often sold realer (and more expensive) time than he actually needs.

From the manufacturer's viewpoint, in most real-time systems the computer is optimized for a single class of tasks. An airline reservation computer was one of the first real-time systems. It had to give each operator answers to questions about seat availability within seconds, then book the resulting reservations and make sure no other operator was simultaneously selling the same seats. A real-time accounts receivable system, on the other hand, may be perfectly adequate if it spits out the requested information within ten minutes. A real-time satellite control system must react within microseconds to keep its vehicle in a proper orbit.

On-line is most easily translated: "on the telephone line."

No more, no less. Nothing could be more boring than listening while a salesman reads his 70-page technical proposal to you over the phone. Similarly, on-line computing is best suited to problems with rather low quantities of printout, unless the priorities justify the cost. Furthermore, just as people on the telephone respond more or less alertly according to their own feelings and personalities, computers differ in the quality of their on-line response. So do bureaus.

Conversational means just what it says.

On-line systems do not necessarily include conversation between the user and the computer. They may be all one way or the other. In real-time applications, the inputs and outputs may be impulses to a satellite motor or readings from a counter in an oil field. Conversation, which is particularly nice for developing new computer programs, is usually implied in "time sharing."

Time sharing means that a number of different people are using a computer at one time, often doing different tasks.

Although most time-sharing computers work on-line to their users, the telephone connection is not a necessary part of the time-sharing system. Several small systems are available from such reputable companies as Digital Equipment Corporation or Hewlett-Packard for in-house time-sharing installations. In these systems, each terminal can be wired directly to the central computer from its location somewhere else in the same building or complex.

The most important thing about time sharing is that it closes the gap between the computer and the end user. Simple languages have been developed for most time-sharing computers. These (often derived from BASIC or FORTRAN) let users pose their problems or ask their questions in simple English. If the computer doesn't understand some word, or finds errors in the instructions it has been given, it says so, usually immediately (or *interactively*), while the user can remember what he really meant to do or say. Most time-sharing terminals are based on the old-fashioned, noisy, inexpensive, and familiar Teletype. Faster (and more expensive) terminals resemble electric typewriters, while others (still more expensive) have TV screens and/or magnetic tape cassettes.

When you close the loop between the user and his computer, the results are sometimes startling. Programmers working through time-sharing terminals are considerably more productive than those using batch systems. Even so, the real benefits are not in instructions-per-week, but in the automation of tasks that require intimate understanding of noncomputer matters. The ages-old problem of telling the programmer how the job should be done no longer exists when the programmer is not intruding between the user and his computer.

In 1967, while commercial time sharing was still in its infancy, a Los Angeles lithographer wrote a program to do a job that IBM and hordes of other computer experts had told him could not be done—calculating printing estimates. Understanding the various grades and types of paper in common use, the machines in his plant, the habits and preferences and prejudices of his printers, and the normal patterns of demand in his business, he built a fairly small database of current prices for the commonly used supplies and products. Then he wrote a rather untidy little program that let him ask the time-sharing system to make the required calculations, leaving himself plenty of room to handle special situations in a "calculator" mode. The average quotation could be run through this system in about half an hour instead of taking him a full day. He quickly found that customers, instead of demanding that he come to their offices, were coming into his office to watch the terminal spit out its quotes. They also began asking questions that grew into little simulation runs. "What if I use the 16-lb. uncoated paper?" "What if we add two-color for the center spread?" The printer and his intuitive understanding of his business remained an integral part of the system.

Remote-batch processing has a number of permutations, but all of them entail sending classic batches of work to the computer over telephone lines.

In essence, batch processing means jobs are tidily lined up and fed through the computer one-at-a-time, often arranged in the order that is most convenient for the computer, rather than for the user. Some of the giant number-crunching computers are now so fast that batch-feeding them still gives very rapid results. In time-sharing systems, many jobs are shuffled in and out of the central processor (the computing part of the computer) at such a rate that each user feels the computer is all his and is working for him right now. It's a pleasant feeling, one that is made possible by the high speed at which the software shunts zeros and ones around in the innards of the machines.

In remote batch, the user feeds his batch of work through telephone lines into the computer, from a terminal or card reader or some other input device on his own premises. Results for fairly large jobs can typically be fed back within less than half an hour. They usually come back on a line printer that is part of the user's remote-batch terminal. Large printouts can also be handled (less expensively) on fast line printers at the computer center if a delay or special delivery is acceptable. This is sometimes called *remote job entry*, though purists prefer to use the term to refer to the situation in which a small input from a small terminal initiates a larger job from data and programs already stored in the central system.

Another phrase that sometimes clutters computer conversations is *three-dimensional,* which was originally GE's own name for the three kinds of service available on its 600 series computers—a combination of local batch, remote batch, and time sharing. Since GE became the nearest analogy that the time-sharing industry has to an IBM in the computer industry, the phrase came into general use, like Nabisco's "shredded wheat." After Honeywell bought GE's computer manufacturing business, the Honeywell 6000 computer was announced as "four-dimensional," having the other three facilities plus *transaction processing.* (This amounts to making a virtue of real-time necessity.) Transaction processing means the computer also has software that makes it cheap and easy to send in such things as invoices or inventory changes as they happen, rather than using old-fashioned, cumbersome pieces of paper. Other modern computers also handle this kind of work.

So much for jargon. The essence of teleprocessing is to realize that *you pay for the speed of response.* Although postal rates are rising fast everywhere, a letter is still cheaper than a telegram, which is cheaper than a phone call, over long distances (in most countries). But if you need an instant answer or a local one, the phone call is often most cost effective.

THE CORPORATION'S NEEDS

In the typical large company, there is room for the entire spectrum of services. Batch work is still the majority. Some sort of remote-batch capability helps coordinate work for divisions that are geographically spread. (Eventually data communication will allow plants to be located without respect to proximity to the parent or other closely related corporate entities.) Some kind of conversational facility with the remote-batch makes it possible to prepare programs and files from a terminal. This is particularly useful if it fits together modules of programs already written.

Although time sharing has been called "ten times as important as the invention of the computer itself" by a leading cybernetician, it is seldom viable economically or technically in a large corporation unless it comes with batch capabilities.

Finally, for some kinds of companies, a graphics ability may be useful. However, the systems that do fancy drawing and computer-aided design tend to gobble up huge quantities of expensive computer time. Two or three graphics users can saturate a system overnight, so graphics is likely to be a luxury unless a dedicated system justifies itself.

One large company kept track of its user population for several months in 1971 on a triple-threat system. Of the commercial users, 65 percent used pure batch, 30 percent used remote job entry, and 5 percent used pure time sharing, which had just been added. Of the scientific users, 20 percent used pure batch, 50 percent used remote job entry, and 30 percent already used the pure time sharing.

"Remote operation is already here," says superuser Philip Dorn. "It requires restructuring of traditional ways of doing things. When they can't see the user, they can't hand him a memo saying 'The machine will be down from one to two tomorrow afternoon.'"

IN-HOUSE/OUT-HOUSE BUREAUS

The service bureau concept is as old as the computer itself. When card-sorting systems came into vogue, in fact, some users who had invested in the new equipment and the people to work it immediately offered spare time to their colleagues in other companies. This in-house/out-house type of bureau still proliferates, and will continue to do so as long as computer managers are able to add and subtract. The appeal is tremendous:

> "If we sell ten hours a week, I'll be able to get that extra disk we've been asking for."
>
> "Bloggs is already using the system 30 hours a week. When we get the new multiprogramming system, we'll sell him a remote terminal and we won't have his people cluttering up the place."
>
> "If we run the computer 24 hours a day instead of eight, it obviously costs one-third as much."

Ergo, another in-house/out-house bureau is born—and, inexorably, a new set of problems for the company.

First of all, even more than when it made the decision to buy a computer, the company is diversifying into the computer business. If it is determined to offer computer services to outsiders, it must begin competing with the growing ranks of serious bureaus. This means it has to have highly trained staff and professional project management. It must be able to meet the deadline it promises. It must deal with yet another set of demanding users. When your own company's fate hinges on the computer, it's bad enough, but what about the client company's fate? In other words, marketing and management skills are usually the scarce items for these ventures, not technical skills.

For the users and providers alike, the paramount problem with an in-house/out-house bureau is the priority question. The computer crashed last night in the middle of Bloggs's payroll run. The repairman came this morning when our own was supposed to be run. The computer finally went up again at noon, and both payrolls are due out at 1 PM. Which set of employees do we disappoint?

This kind of question bedevils any computer department from time to time. But within a single company, ages-old communication channels and unwritten priorities are often sufficient to cope with each crisis on an ad hoc basis. The in-house department can offer a "July special on programming" to its internal departments to keep workloads balanced. Similarly, a pure computer bureau that understands survival has developed backup capabilities, charging structures, and skills for dealing gently with irate clients. The fledgling in-house/out-house bureau often seems to have all the disadvantages of both, and none of the advantages.

Historically, these minibureaus do not survive in the larval stage for long. If such a venture is successful in its early offerings to an eager public, it usually takes the bureau business seriously enough to spin off like a butterfly from the parent organization. Such a bureau often assumes separate corporate coloration, though it works from an assured base of business from the parent. The aircraft and aerospace companies have generally gone in this direction, with mixed results. One of the largest examples is Boeing Computer Services, Inc., which started life in 1970 with $100 million worth of computers, about 3000 people, and the expectation of about $100 million per year in business from the Boeing Company.

More often, the in-house/out-house bureau settles down to earth, becoming a centralized computer operation for its own company. This kind of bureau can be quite effective when it "sells" its services on a competitive basis to other departments of the company, who begin to recognize that the computer, too, must work on a profit-and-loss basis. If there is spare time, this can be sold on a regular basis to a few friendly firms.

A few of these corporate bureaus, especially in such fields as engineering, find that the applications they have developed for departments in their own companies are actually better than commercially available software—a natural and happy result when computer people have intimate knowledge of the user's business. The decision to offer such specialized software on a service bureau basis has broad competitive implications; it also requires sufficient documentation and training so outside end-users can use it effectively. But the computer business is singularly open in this respect. These specialist in-house/out-house bureau services or software ventures often thrive in their quiet corners.

TIME-SHARING BUREAUS

Time sharing suffered the unfortunate fate of becoming a fad in the late sixties, not only among would-be bureau entrepreneurs but also on Wall Street. As developments at Dartmouth, MIT, Manchester, and several other universities began to filter outside, people who were less academic began to envisage a terminal in every home, calculating the shopping list, transmitting transactions to and fro for the cashless, checkless society, and easing the poor overworked housewife's lot still further.

Fortunately, the predictions of a terminal in every home did not come to fruition. The predictors failed to consider human resistance to change (and the high cost of terminals). Those who were doing the envisaging tended to overestimate their markets by a factor sometimes approaching infinity. So for several wild years it was possible for any company with a name like Snooks Time Sharing Corporation to raise several million dollars from a public that was considerably more sensible about whether it wanted terminals in its own kitchens than it was about where its investment money went.

The computer makers underestimated the time-sharing phenomenon almost as much as the entrepreneurs overestimated it. First, the manufacturers thought it would never work, even though it was already working on machines they had sold to the universities. Next, they decided it would never sell. Finally, they began to take notice as a few pioneer bureaus started to tune up their machines and create workable software for commercial time sharing. This is no easy task when you are shuffling 40 users around in the space that used to accommodate one.) Software was (and still is) the biggest headache and the biggest expense for a time-sharing company. Slow off the mark, most of the computer manufacturers didn't really offer workable time-sharing software/hardware combinations until 1971.

Like other Wall Street fads, time sharing was destined to go through exuberant growth and overgrowth, then a settling-down period in which attrition and amalgamation would weed out the losers and result in a fairly sound new industry. Unfortunately, the recession that began in 1969 came at exactly the wrong moment for the fledgling industry. For many time-sharing companies, their machines and people were still going through the tuning-up and settling-down stages. Their software was just beginning to work, and many technical whiz kids had succumbed to the temptation to add just a few extra elegant embellishments. Users had not quite flocked to the time-sharing bureaus at the predicted rates, though the overall volume was increasing at a steady and healthy pace. Suddenly, the additional capital that many of these companies needed to achieve the elusive break-even point dried up completely.

For many, the result was bankruptcy. In fairness, most of them went to considerable trouble to make sure their clients received adequate service elsewhere, even donating special programs to better-financed erstwhile competitors. Changing can be a fairly simple matter when the user simply dials a different telephone number, but it is nonetheless inconvenient, since each time-sharing computer seems to speak a slightly different dialect and demand a slightly different protocol. Though the existing users were inconvenienced during this phase, most of them kept right on using time-sharing services, and the amount of use continued to grow every month. A few companies began to buy their own time-sharing computers for in-house use. (Most of these, incidentally, still supplement the in-house service with bureaus.)

The main damage from the 1969-70 bubble-bursting was a loss in time-sharing credibility. The successful users had no reason to broadcast their satisfaction. Though the technique and languages were improving rapidly, people who had never used time sharing—many of them experienced DP people—read gloomy financial reports and bankruptcy notices rather than glowing user reports. Many companies are still reluctant to try time sharing.

This is one instance in which the cost is very low, and so are the initial risks—at least to the user, if not the bureau. A single Teletype terminal, with all the modifications and telephone gear it needs for time sharing, can cost as little as $75-100 per month. Bureau prices vary according to location, specialization, and other competitive factors, but a few hours a month can give any company a taste of time sharing for about $100 more.

The peril is obvious. Your people will like it. Like eating only a few salted peanuts, it takes too much willpower to remain a minimum user. Honeywell estimates that the average user in Britain (where time-sharing charges are higher than in the United States) spends about £250 to £300 per month per terminal. In the United States the figure seems to have settled down fairly steadily to about $500 per terminal per month. Usage per terminal tends to rise slightly as people get more skilled, but at the same time, they learn how to tidy up their early programs and use the time-sharing facilities more economically.

Addiction to time sharing can lead to uncontrolled use, which gets not only expensive but inefficient. Some measure of control is usually worthwhile. Plessey, Ltd., says that a terminal in practical terms only serves people within a 20-yard radius. Plessey's "natural" control is keeping the terminal population low, so users have to queue up for access. Though this seems to defeat part of the purpose of time sharing, it keeps frivolous use to a minimum.

Raytheon, Inc., using more than a dozen time-sharing services near Boston, has instituted a rather elaborate control system in which a central department handles training in the languages and services available, then teaches users which service to use for which kind of task. Raytheon shuffles all users through a central switchboard where pertinent details of their usage are logged and later analyzed so the balance of services can be adjusted to the demand, or vice versa.

The benefit in time sharing is not so much instant response for applications that used to take a long time, nor even an improvement in programmer output. Instead, it is the ability to do things that could not previously be done, like the Los Angeles lithographer's bidding program. It is hard to quantify this kind of benefit, but in every technical conference you now find a sprinkling of papers or speeches about new and often very sensible tasks that have been done or are regularly being done by nonprogrammers using time-sharing terminals.

COMPUTER UTILITIES

For all its blessings, pure time-sharing service has turned out to be a mixed blessing for the proprietor of the system. After a few perilous years of managing intense software development, fighting off headhunting competitors, placating irate users (because every crash is instantly visible to every one of those simultaneous users who feels the computer is all his own), dodging creditors, wooing investors, and learning to live with his ulcer, the time-sharing entrepreneur can look forward to operating slightly in the black (if he has captured a large enough share of the market)—until competitive pressures force him to invest in a newer, bigger machine or data communications system, and start the process all over again.

Survival is much more likely for the computer utility, which offers computer power over telephone lines as if it were water, electricity, or transport—at whatever speed and concentration the user demands and is willing to pay for. This is the triple (or quadruple) threat combination of local and remote batch processing plus conversation. Some utilities also offer specialized programs, databanks, or transaction services at an additional premium or per-transaction charge.

University Computing Corporation (UCC) set up one of the first, largest, and "purest" utility services. Scattering giant Univac 1108 computers around the world, UCC let users do what they would with the resulting power. Another UCC subsidiary manufactured and sold a range of remote-batch terminals for different-sized users. Yet another (Datran) began work on special data communications network to compete with the telephone company in the United States. Other subsidiaries sold specialized services and databases that worked on the 1108 systems. Clients could use the standard remote-batch terminals that transmitted information very rapidly (up to 4800 bits per second), with fast line printers (up to 800 lines per minute) and card readers (up to 1000 cards per minute). They could also install slow (ten characters per second) Teletype-type terminals that could get access to information on the big number-crunching systems through smaller conversational front-end computers. The conversational system let them use files stored on the remote-batch system. This makes sense, particularly because it restores the feeling of physical ownership of information that is often lost when a card file turns into a computer file.

A computer utility, whether local, national, or worldwide, offers business users a number of conveniences. Fast turnaround has already been mentioned, though the need for this is not obvious on every job. Anyone who wants real-time payroll processing deserves to pay what it costs.

Procedures for doing work through a remote-batch terminal are usually easier than those in a small computer center, even though the amount of work done is often greater. Nor is it necessary to schedule your computer work with the utility, though most of them offer cut rates for clients who call for certain large jobs to be done on a regular basis. You have less worries about hardware and software reliability; they're less likely to fail, and if they do, it's not your worry—you have recourse if they affect your business. Some utilities now allow users to dial a priority, paying accordingly for anything from instant to overnight service.

A bureau is a business too. Therefore there will be times when things go wrong. With several thousand in the United States and several hundred in Britain to choose from, there are enough bureaus so that it should never be necessary to put up with a long succession of crashes and excuses. On the other hand, a workable relationship with a businesslike bureau should not be allowed to founder over one or two minor disasters. Many companies have enough work of different kinds to justify workable relationships with several bureaus, which allows costs and specialties to be optimized, and can still give the user himself a fall-back position if new staff, software, or equipment causes too many problems at the primary bureau.

SPECIALIZED BUREAUS

Specialized bureaus are as old as in-house/out-house bureaus. They came about the same way—a demand existed for something a company had developed for itself.

Payroll programs, for example, have kept a number of small computers churning profitably for years. One successful bureau does more than 350 payrolls every month, using a modular package that can be tailored to different companies, then batching the payrolls so that they are normally run only once a week. Although many companies make inquiries about special payrolls, the bureau says less than 2 percent actually demand amendments beyond the options that are already available. As with software packages, bureau services are likely to cost more if you demand custom-tailored facilities. Specialized bureaus often cost a bit more than general bureaus, on a per-hour basis, but they are already likely to have programs with most of the features you want. They are also likely to have consultants, systems analysts, and programmers with the most pertinent experience for your problem—even your payroll.

The trend to bureau specialization is growing stronger, and the range of specialties is also growing—inventory control, portfolio analysis, insurance, engineering, accounting, library information retrieval, advertising, management sciences, construction. As each bureau finds its particular niche in an industry or over a range of applications, the user has a better choice of competent services for each task.

Many have programs of considerable sophistication, which would be very expensive and time consuming to develop in-house. For instance, in the manufacturing field, a thumbnail sketch of a cost-effective bureau service may be helpful. Lowndes-Ajax Computer Services near London spent several years developing IBM's CLASS (Capacity Loading And Scheduling System) to fit its own computer and customers. This is a set of programs for requirements planning, inventory control, order control, costing, and scheduling and loading.

CLASS is usually run for customers on a batch basis over the weekend, so they receive fresh reports every Monday morning. There is nothing particularly glamorous or impressive about it, except that it works, and that it can be used on a bureau basis from IBM itself, Lowndes-Ajax, or several others. Lowndes-Ajax says the file organization (based on IBM's BOMP) is the most critical portion of the entire job. Figure 11-1 shows a simplified diagram of the various departments (shown in boxes) that are involved in these applications; the paperwork between them (shown in circles); and how the different segments of the package (shown by dotted lines) overlap and interact.

The files for the system are organized with item masters (unique records for each part) and a product structure, which shows the relation-

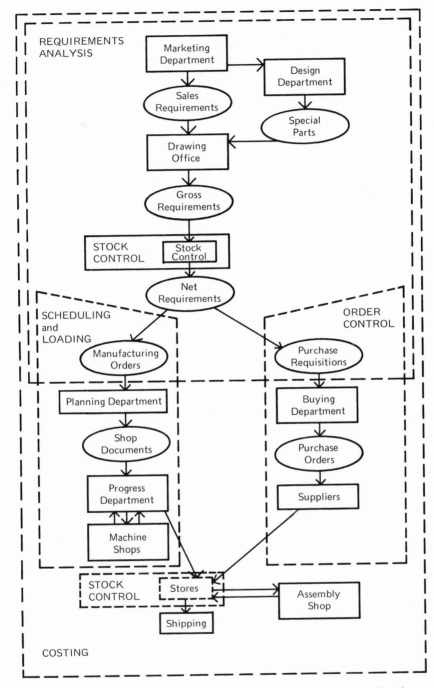

Fig. 11-1. Flow of information for a manufacturing control application.

ships between parts. Thus, simplistically, if product A is made up of two B's, one C, and four D's, and part B in turn is made up of five D's and two E's, then the system can take into account the delivery and production cycles and calculate a schedule. So, if you need 100 of product A in period 4, it would produce the following table:

PART \ PERIOD	1	2	3	4
A				100
B			200	
C			100	
D		1000	400	
E		400		

This is the gross requirement. Subtracting from it the inventory on hand (less safety stock) and adding to it the firm orders gives a net requirement. Taking into account lead times, shrinkage or scrap allowances, and other routine factors makes the requirements analysis portion alone a fairly complicated matter.

The inventory control portion of the package is similarly complex. But inventory control gives a tremendous payoff. It has been estimated in Britain that stock in inventory often equals four times the total overdraft (bank credit) of the company. Using an automated control system can eventually cut these levels down.

The computer cannot get rid of obsolete or overstocked items, so inventory levels often rise initially. Once the slow movers are properly balanced (which can take as long as a year), a reduction on the order of 10 percent can reasonably be expected, even from a very simple system.

The order control portion of the suite leads on from inventory control to watch over purchase orders, sales orders, and factory orders. It is probably most effective in a streamlined version that depends on exception reports rather than huge, detailed printouts. This elementary but sensible approach lets you expedite the orders that are late and ignore the others. You can also request regular reports on selected orders if you don't feel that hopeful and trusting about their timely arrival.

The costing portion of the manufacturing suite accumulates labor, materials, and overhead costs for each product. The ability to make temporary changes that don't affect the basic files means you can do sensitivity analyses, looking at the effect of different labor rates, procedures, or suppliers, or "playing the market."

Finally, the scheduling and loading portion shows whether you are wasting manpower or equipment, or where more may be needed. It produces such reports as a schedule list, work center load analyses for 1 to 12 weeks or 1 to 10 days, and the value of work in progress. Another list shows which jobs should be done first, second, and so on, for each machine, with the due date of the job as the first determinant. Work in progress is expensive. Furthermore, if you can control it better, your sales are likely to improve because your deliveries will improve.

"We wouldn't recommend implementing all five parts of the system simultaneously, even on a bureau basis," says a Lowndes-Ajax specialist. "It's much better if you go one at a time, and take the opportunity to clean up your files as you go. Then go on to the next part a few months later."

IBM and Lowndes-Ajax have collected statistics from some companies that use these systems from bureaus. Increased throughput ranges from 10 to 40 percent—that means factory throughput, not computer throughput. Reduced lead time is reported at 33 percent for one German company (which cut its lead time from nine months to six months and increased its on-time deliveries from 65 to 92 percent). Work-in-progress reductions were reported from 10 to 45 percent. Reduced idle time on the floor was harder to establish, but most companies reported a major reduction in the number and duration of production meetings.

The computer men do not attribute all these benefits to their machines and software. "Ten percent of the overall improvement may be due to the new psychological discipline," says Lowndes-Ajax. "Using a computer this way is a form of faith-healing."

The bureau system for manufacturing probably works best if the user has one good man bridging the chasm between the shop floor and the computer. The machine cannot talk to people in the shop with four-letter expletives.

OVERSELL, OVERBUY, OVERFLOW, AND OVERKILL

The computer manufacturers themselves have been edging into the bureau business with increased fervor, though IBM is unable to offer bureau services directly in the United States because of antitrust agreements. Control Data Corporation has already set up a large network on a utility basis, and the tentacles of the Honeywell time-sharing and remote-batch network are spreading around the world, while GE continues to be the largest vendor in the United States. On most of these networks, information from branches in many cities or countries can be stored in a single location, and used from anywhere else, even though the user pays only local telephone charges.

Control Data was the first to admit tacitly that computer makers had been guilty of "oversell." Though CDC referred only to the company's desire to help users avoid their tendency to "overbuy," the initial network announcement implied clearly that CDC's computer salesmen would be encouraged to sell their customers somewhat smaller computers, and then help them find the applications that could overflow onto CDC's utility-type network.

Using a bureau for overflow makes good economic sense, whether it is a stopgap measure or a permanent arrangement. It is also convenient to be able to use the same type of machine you have in your own installation. For many applications, though, this is an unnecessary luxury, especially where standard programs are already available. Shop around. You have more choices than the computer salesman is likely to reveal.

Even here, caveat emptor. Computer sales people and bureau sales people, too, tend to be skilled in giving helpful advice on how to computerize applications. They are constitutionally less able to advise users *not* to computerize applications. Unless you're careful, you'll find an on-line real-time conversational terminal in the executive bathroom.

For many users, the cheapest form of data transmission is still the automobile.

12

Communicating Data

When you take your car out of the garage, you can park it on the public street in front of your house. Then you can drive it anywhere on a network of roads that covers the entire country, or the world, for that matter —meandering dirt roads, ill-kempt secondary lanes, one-way streets through towns, heavily traveled truck routes, enormous intertwined superhighways stretching between major cities.

Whether you use a bureau or your own computer system, data communications should provide you similar networks for your data traffic. The country lanes that suffice for casual use in your car are analogous to the voice telephone network, which can be used for some data as well. But picture a dirt road that has suddenly become a main thoroughfare. That is the current situation for data users on the voice network. It was not designed for the frequency and duration patterns of data calls; in some cities these are putting an insupportable strain on the system for the telephone companies and the regular users as well.

A few data superhighways already exist, and plans for others are fairly advanced. The real problem will be to improve the network of local access roads to and from these superhighways. Like the roads, the telephone system is regarded as a national resource in most countries, and is controlled very closely. Thus bureaucracy will impede rapid progress, but the user's interests will take some precedence, as long as these interests are communicated to the overseeing bodies.

THE PURVEYORS

As in Britain, America's phone system is a monopoly. American Telephone & Telegraph ("the Bell System") is in truth a collection of smaller telephone companies that have gathered under the AT&T flag, but that have not yet completed the emotional aspects of their amalgamation. AT&T is under the jurisdiction of the Federal Communications Commission, which, in mid-1971, after several years of study, surprised AT&T by declaring an end to monopoly on several fronts. No longer were users prohibited from installing non-Bell ("foreign") equipment at their own ends of a telephone line. This gave computer users new alternatives for data communications equipment. Even more important, the FCC finally ruled that unregulated carriers, notably two large new companies named Datran and Microwave Communications, Inc. (MCI), would be permitted to compete with AT&T in providing lower-cost services to transmit computer-related information. In December 1971 a few companies began using MCI's new microwave network from Saint Louis to Chicago. Almost simultaneously, AT&T announced that it would drop the rates on more heavily used routes between major cities in the United States.

Though data communications amounted to $500 million revenue for AT&T in 1970, this was just 10 per cent of Bell's total revenues. Looking at it another way, less than 10 percent of all the data that arrives at U.S. computers gets there by data communications. More than 90 percent is still carried by messengers or postmen. This ratio itself will change, and companies are simply generating more information in the seventies. AT&T anticipates that there may be as much as $5 billion per year in data traffic alone by 1980.

THE POTENTIAL

Isaac Auerbach (futurologist to the computer industry) expresses grave doubts about data communications, which could so easily repeat the computer mistakes of the past. "We have the same potential here," he says. "But it is possible to make a similar size mess. If we are smart, we will take advantage of those mistakes and not repeat them with data communications." Auerbach believes that many of the problems of computer use came from the mistaken notion that the computer was or should be a universal machine. "In data communications, a terminal, for example, cannot have universal application. The techniques should be different for different applications. What was designed for the military cannot be shoehorned into the commercial environment. But there will be pressure on the computer-communications network to force-fit universality it was not designed for."

It is becoming clear that the communications-based information system *can* do many useful things for the companies that know how to use it. It can be used effectively to rationalize or disperse large companies, for example. Whether the company chooses to centralize or decentralize, a network can enhance the task. To centralize the information flow, you simply replace the smaller computers in provincial outposts with remote-batch terminals, which usually include card readers and line printers to handle transmission to and from the faraway center. These can also incorporate low-cost minicomputers that permit some calculations or verification of the input to be performed locally. Adding "local storage" in the form of core or disk memory to this kind of remote terminal allows it to stand alone for many applications and still send in its information as required to the corporate headquarters or other elements of the company. This approach could eventually mean that geography is no longer a limitation; closely related departments could be widely separated and still exchange information effectively.

As companies get bigger and more complex, it is not necessarily the case that they need more *accurate* information (though most computer people would stoutly maintain they do). Instead, they are much more likely to need more *consistent* information. On the industrial side, the part numbers, for example, feed not only into the manufacturing system but also into the accounting system; standardization and centralization mean that similar components for related products should be identified and grouped. In accounting, information from one subsidiary must be related to information from another, so the results that are fed through the management hierarchy mean something. This is where the computer-based information system, properly used, can be helpful.

A major achievement of the lunar exploration program in the United States was getting thousands of people in hundreds of companies to work together. The biggest problem was the concentration and dispersal of information. Here were sown the seeds of management information systems.

Management information, in real, earthbound life, needs to be *on-time*, not real-time or on-line. Like the reports used for the moon program, it is usually the consistency rather than the extreme accuracy that gives such information value. This is where data communications can help. At Boeing, for example, when incoming goods arrive, a teleprocessing system sends simultaneous and identical notifications to the accounting department, the inventory control group, the warehouse, and other groups that are waiting for the particular materials. This system uses data communications for speed and consistency, but all the groups involved are within a five-mile radius. It is a purely operational system, not a management information system. But the payoff is high: it saves several days and frees millions in capital that would be tied up in additional inventory if a conventional reporting system were used.

Changes in management hierarchies also demand changes in the information flow. Russell McFall, chairman of Western Union in the United States, points out that the ability to manage a successful business is much more dependent on outside forces now. "The concept of the information revolution hasn't helped much," he comments wryly. "Companies fall into two classes: those who are standing and waiting for the revolution to come, and those who feel it's already here. In either case, they may find they have created a monument to technological feasibility that is really a business dinosaur."

"Like many other companies," says McFall, "we have gone from being a small, single-product company to being a large, diversified, multiproduct, multimarket corporation. Our customers are more demanding today. The numbers of decisions we have to make increase. The impact of each decision is growing. And we have less time in which to make them. Without an information system, this is much more difficult."

McFall points out, too, that the president seldom comes up through the ranks any more. Today's professional manager has not grown up with the business; more often he is brought in from outside at the top level. So he needs an information system all the more.

Data communications can keep an organization from becoming a dinosaur. Despite growth, companies can still react rapidly, with human-scale reflexes. Allied Bakeries in Britain, for example, distributes bread, cake, and candies from about 50 bakeries through a low-cost network of off-line paper tape inputs, connected to five small computer bureaus. These handle the daily orders from 70,000 customer shops and 2500 of Allied's own shops. Routine amendments to the orders are sent in between 4:00 and 6:00 each evening; emergency changes can be handled up until 6 AM when the 5000 vans roll out to begin their daily deliveries. According to Gerry Fisher who heads data processing for Allied's parent (Associated British Foods), this kind of job would be impossible without the data communications system. On the other hand, Fisher points out that from a business point of view, it would be absurd to put expensive on-line terminals into the bakeries or shops when off-line paper tape can do the job quite adequately.

DOS AND DON'TS

There are a number of things that data communications should *not* be expected to do for a company. Like the computer to which it connects, the data communications system cannot be the brain of the company, only the network of nerves along which the impulses flow to the center. The flaw in many communications-based information systems is that they attempt to do too much of the corporate thinking; failure in any one realm tends to throw doubt upon all the rest of the reports or capabilities of the system. There is a major difference between the systems that are used for operational purposes and those that are applied to management decision making. The notable successes are those that attack the operational side. The brain (or the management information system) builds up its knowledge of the outside world from the inputs it gets from its successful operational systems, whether they be sights and sounds or bakery orders and job cards.

No company can justify the cost of transmitting information for planning its future operations. Occasionally this kind of information can be a convenient by-product. Yet this is often the first application that is force-fitted to a communications system. Companies still fail to recognize that they don't need equipment working at the speed of light to handle information about long-term growth. As Russell McFall points out, "There are days we spend all our time slicing information with a razor blade and dishing it out with a shovel."

A few simple rules of thumb for data communications thread their way through the case histories that are already available:

1. *Start at the top.* If you get the priorities right to begin with, the cost will be much lower and the system is more likely to accomplish what you expect of it. McFall says: "The most successful systems are the ones where the top managers spent time in the conceptual design phase. These are the people best suited to sitting down and documenting the seven or

eight kinds of information each one needs to do his own job." Without top management interest at this stage, people tend to design information systems without considering the communications systems and vice versa. The administrative people and the DP people optimize their respective systems, but when you put them together you don't get an optimized information system. Going back to optimize it later is hyperexpensive.

2. *Start with the organization.* A streamlined communications-based information system may be useless if it must be used to serve a bulky vertical hierarchy. Similarly, an inflexible data communications system may render impossible (or overexpensive) otherwise sensible organizational changes. Yet another aspect of the organization seldom gets enough attention: the place of data communications itself. The data communications manager ought to be a high-level executive who understands the flow of information throughout the organization; instead, in most companies, he is a telephone technician who has been elevated from his corner within the facilities group simply because he is the only one in the company able to talk to the "mysterious" people from the telephone company.

3. *Start early.* Speaking of the telephone company, it needs to know as early as possible when a company is planning a major communications system. Even though it may be several years before such a system is implemented, if the telephone company is involved at the earliest planning stages, it can offer useful suggestions—like locating your center away from the downtown area, where there are too few telephone lines available. It can also amend its own planning in time to have ready the facilities you will need. The most elegant system in the world won't work for the five extra months it takes to get the leased lines you ordered; carrying the salaries of the resident information experts for that span won't be comfortable. Similarly, within your own company, it is not only necessary to know the technology and to apply it, it is also necessary to educate people and restructure the organization. If plans for the system are widely discussed long before it is installed, there will be less resistance to the new standards and procedures it imposes. And many of these can be introduced long before the system itself demands them.

4. *Start slow.* The most common management complaints about data communications systems, like computer systems before them, deal with technical people underestimating the time and money involved. Invariably this means that as time runs out the technical people have to cut corners and make desperate patchwork compromises in order to meet the deadlines. Most companies so far have burned their fingers on data communi-

cations because they spent too much time and money trying to convert such large failures to large successes (with little success). If you start with small successes, you have a much better chance to build them gradually together into larger successes. Some useful databanks have been built from combinations of smaller databanks. You don't have to do this all at once, but you have to design from the beginning with the possibility in mind, to keep the system flexible. A large success takes years, not weeks or months.

5. *Start in your own field.* The 1969-70 bureau failures are dramatic examples of the perils of venturing into large data communications networks outside of your own sphere of interest. In many cases, technically competent groups underestimated not the communications challenge but the time and resources it would take to create a service in a business outside their own. The success stories are different. A number of smaller distributors, for example, started file systems in their own fields, then went on to learn about computers. Some of them are beginning to share their small communications systems and databases now.

Systems to assist management can also be blended with external systems to satisfy customer demands. In one very simple system for retail outlets in the United States, the stores transmitted their bank deposit details to the central computer, which processed them and transferred the deposits directly to the bank computer. This not only speeded up record-keeping, but it also speeded cash flow by 50 percent and freed up to two million dollars in operating capital.

The "successful" examples all share one feature: high payoff, not in the far future, but right away, at the operational level.

The technologists themselves are beginning to realize that their machines and systems have reached an outer limit of complexity. The limit is not the speed of light nor the ability to dissipate heat, but the tolerance of nontechnologists. Commander Grace Hopper, one of the world's first computer programmers, has a pleasant scenario for simpler computer/communications systems in the future. These would be made up of clusters of cheap and reliable minicomputers, each with a separate telephone number. The salesman entering his orders pushes a "Sales" button on his office terminal, which automatically routes the call to the phone number of the sales miniprocessor. Some information from that transaction is automatically fed to the delivery minicomputer, while other items are fed to the management modeling system. Meanwhile, the requisite paperwork for the salesman himself is sent back to his terminal a few minutes later, and the invoicing clerk receives a notification on yet another terminal. There is no operating system, no software bugs (very little software), no air-conditioning, no nonsense. If something goes wrong with one minicomputer or telephone line, you use another while the bad one is being fixed.

Many of these systems can be implemented now, using regular telephone lines. But voice-grade lines are both unreliable and expensive for large volumes of data communications. It is wasteful to have a 200-mph Ferrari bogged down in a traffic jam on a dirt road.

Private leased lines are usually a good investment if you can justify the higher speed or higher volume traffic. If your needs are actually quite simple, like the daily orders for the bakery, don't overlook the benefits of off-line (batched, rather than immediate) transmission of paper tape or even magnetic tape from cassettes.

Eventually, national and international networks for data communication can be taken for granted as easily as we accept the highway system today. In the meantime, patience, top management consideration, and close coordination with the people at the telephone company are a user's first lines of action for better data communications.

13

Finding and Keeping People

No matter how powerful your car is, how safe, how well maintained, how finely tuned, it won't go very fast if you let Aunt Susie drive it, and it may never get where it's supposed to be going if you lend it to your teenage neighbor.

Good driving is just as crucial in computing. Dr. Hal Sackman of the University of Southern California says that comparisons between good and bad programmers using the same computer system can be quantified, with differences as much as 60:1 in productivity. In Britain, cybernetician Stafford Beer reports similar comparisons between good and bad programmers. Taking the best as a unit of one, his study revealed that the worst programmers took 26 times as long to debug their programs, 10 times as much computer time, and 25 times as much coding time—their code was 5 times larger, and their running times were 15 times as long.

In financial terms, this could mean you would need at least 10 times as much computer power (though you might be able to get away with only 5 times as much storage) if your installation were staffed only with bad programmers. Or, looking at it another way, you may already be paying for much more computer than you should, simply because you have a mediocre group filling it up as fast as you can upgrade.

If this is the penalty for having poor programmers, what does it cost you to have mediocre systems analysts? They affect not only the computer but the speed and efficiency with which things happen in every other department. A poor DP manager not only carries responsibility for all these terrors, but can also perpetuate the problem by hiring more mediocrities.

Fortunately the corollary is true—if you have one of the best DP managers, he may attract a few really good programmers and systems analysts. These treasures are all rare, but worth searching for.

WHERE TO FIND THEM

There is a growing (and sometimes rueful) consensus that the *data processing manager* had better be a manager, not a technician. Most DP managers during the sixties were former programmers who had wafted through the ranks as systems analysts until they were one day tapped for the top computer position. Few had business training or pertinent experience in hiring and motivating people, much less scheduling the use of human or inhuman resources. This unfortunate lack has led to the isolation of many computer departments from the mainstream of corporate life.

One of the best places to find potential DP managers is within the management of your own company. SKF, the Swedish multinational manufacturer, keeps a computerized database on its top 2200 managers around the world. They are shuffled around to keep a balance between specific skills and between local and nonnational management in each country. A list like that would contain many potential DP managers. A good manager from a user department within the company usually enjoys the challenge of learning about computers, and handles his eventual department in a businesslike way. Training a technical man in the nuances of management at senior levels is a much more difficult task, though that has been the classic approach. Once more, the awful fog of computer jargon must take some of the blame.

It often boils down to a make-or-buy decision. Hiring a first-class DP manager from outside can be an expensive proposition. I have never met one who wasn't willing to listen to an offer, but the candidates you want are men who have grown in stature until they are included in corporate management to a considerable extent. Only very spectacular offers are liable to dislodge them from their secure and rewarding nests.

Somewhere in between making a DP manager and buying one is the consultant-turned-DP-manager. Many capable men in the course of their management careers (particularly the ones who started out with technical specialties) spend a few years with a consultancy. They feel this gives them breadth and exposure to more management problems than they might encounter in a single company. It amounts to on-the-job graduate-level training with superb pay. But after a few years of advising rather than implementing, many would be happy to return to industry in a challenging position (such as running-up a run-down DP department). They are attracted by a chance to make visible improvement and be closely involved in the progress of the company. Consulting salaries are often a trifle inflated, and such men can sometimes be enticed by reasonable offers as long as the position carries stature within your company. Very few are willing to accept a direct reduction in salary.

Executive headhunters can help you find a DP manager. There are a few that specialize in computer executives. They can place advertisements, screen large numbers of people for the handful that fit your corporate style as well as your written specifications, and then they can verify references, salary levels, and so on. They can also be used when you know the head you want to hunt, but it would be impolite to go after the candidate directly. The computer manufacturers themselves have had no-poaching agreements for years, which has led to a thriving business for executive headhunters around New York, Philadelphia, and Minneapolis, to name but a few. An executive headhunter will probably cost you about 20 to 25 percent of the man's first-year salary. Some charge these fees only if they find successful candidates. Others believe the winnowing out of unsuitable candidates is an important part of the overall job of consulting on staffing problems, and charge a retainer equal to some percentage of the usual fee, whether or not they find a winning candidate.

If you are looking for an *information director,* the same problems of supply and demand exist, only they are amplified a hundredfold. Such creatures are almost nonexistent at present. (Two of the 102 companies in the British Institute of Management study in 1970 had computer people at the director level.) The need for a generalist is even greater in this position, which may help ease the problem, because operations research or industrial engineering men who are able to operate at director level do exist within many companies. If the chief executive himself views information as a corporate resource, he may already have attracted the kinds of people who could implement broad policies to make it more useful.

It is seldom possible to go outside with a specification for an information director. An advertisement that spells out the responsibilities may attract highly capable candidates, but they cannot be expected to have seven years of experience in just this kind of position. Information directors will be made, not bought, until at least the early eighties.

Finding *systems analysts* is almost as crucial. Fortunately, standards for systems analyst qualifications are being established on both sides of the Atlantic. There are already a number of systems analysts, first-class ones, who have grown into their present positions before such standards existed, so the absence of formal qualification does not necessarily denote a second-class computing citizen.

In Britain the National Computing Centre training plan for computer systems analysts gives some indication of the qualifications. This starts out with a preliminary three-month period during which students from different backgrounds are prepared for the common basic training. During this time, they take a two-week course in the fundamentals of EDP and another two-week course in business. In the following year, they go through a general course, either to provide basic training for those who have no previous systems analyst training or experience, or to beef up the experience of those who grew into their jobs without formal training. This segment includes a six-week course in systems analysis or a four-week course in systems analysis and design (for the experienced analysts). The final 18-month portion of the curriculum, for trained analysts only, starts with a week-long course in systems documentation standards, flowing into a two-week course on business information systems, one week each on operations research, hardware and software updating, systems evaluation, and finally on-line systems. (Most of these NCC courses are available as packages for in-company use.)

With such tools available, the best place to look for systems analysts is inside your own company. This is one more field in which capable people from user departments who know the company and its ways can be trained in the required computer skills. For a neophyte installation it may be possible to do most of the systems analyst recruiting from inside. If this is started when the original planning for an installation begins, there will be sufficient time to train the first few analysts past the beginner phase before major applications are implemented. The entire task may be easier if you are working with a consultant firm that includes training in its capabilities. In a smaller company it may be necessary to recruit outside for replacements; your own investment in creating a group of good analysts will no doubt benefit other companies that took a different decision at the rent-or-buy point. Though it may take longer for outsiders to learn the company, whether systems analysts are made or bought doesn't seem to have a huge effect on the success of a computer installation itself, according to a McKinsey report.[1] The effect on the company's profits was not so easy to quantify.

The main benefit of in-house recruiting is emotional. In-house recruits are more likely to know their way around, and to avoid stepping on interdepartmental toes. Computers mean change. When the demand to change procedures that are known and familiar comes from a group of strangers, brought in to computerize things, it will meet more resistance than it might from the known and familiar computer department that has been created from inside, with a systems analyst who used to be a member of the department that is being told to change. The analysts are also more likely to be used as communications channels for new ideas from present or potential users.

In addition to knowing the company and knowing the computers, the analyst must be able to talk with managers in noncomputer terms. Whether this skill is already developed, or can be developed with extra training, it is clearly a prerequisite for systems analysts. No matter how capable a man's flow charts, if he can't explain them and discuss them with his own management and the user management, they aren't much use. Too much of his work is human relations within the company and public relations for its computer to entrust this type of job to an abrasive or incoherent person.

Finding *programmers* is a constant strain on every installation because these are people who tend to change jobs easily. Attrition rates between 20 and 33 percent are common in programming departments. During the programmers' heyday in America, the average length of time a programmer stayed with one company was about two years. The advent of harder times has brought a little more stability.

Systems programmers—the ones who write the basic software for the computers—are a particularly rare breed. In the words of Philip Dorn: "We computer people are different, particularly systems programmers. Sometimes I think we need our own personnel men, able to ignore the long hair, beards, and sandals. I don't care about these things; if the kid knows the inside of OS 360, I want him. There's no way to get him through the normal personnel department."

Programmers who specialize in certain applications are also worth their

1. Every couple of years, McKinsey comes up with a report full of horrifying statistics on the world's computer resources that are wasted, misused, or unprofitable. This particular version is called "Unlocking the Computer's Profit Potential," McKinsey & Co., Inc., New York, 1968. The latest version is available to computer users at no charge.

weight in gold (and know it). Both these classes of experienced programmers will probably have to be headhunted. Fortunately there are a number of reputable computer staff agencies who know where such bodies are buried. Their fees, like those of the executive headhunters, are usually pegged to the salary of the successful candidate. Some of them, incidentally, make more from surcharges to the companies for whom they advertise than they do from the actual placement fees. If you already advertise for noncomputer people, you may save money by trying your own advertisement rather than paying a stiff fee to have it done for you by a computer personnel agency. A modest ad in a weekly computer journal is relatively inexpensive compared with a hefty percentage of the applicant's annual salary.

Regular DOS/COBOL programmers (even PL/1 programmers) can also be created from within. The chance to get into computing is very appealing to many young employees, so there is seldom a lack of volunteers. Training can also be extended to outside beginners, with considerable success. One London bureau spent about £1000 per programmer in 1967 to put 50 beginners through a nine-month course (plus the cost of their salaries for that time). Though the £50,000 investment seems excessive at first glance, the result was a well-trained group of programmers, with the specific skills the bureau needed (including real-time programming), relatively low salaries, uniformly high standards, and cohesiveness as a group. More than half were still there four years later, forming a strong backbone for the programming department.

Computing is democratic. The genre is surprisingly free from age, sex, color, or class barriers. If a wizened Zulu warrior of 93 could write workable programs, then get them documented and debugged on time, he could earn a fine living as a programmer. A number of women in modern installations have been able to take terminals home during maternity leave and continue doing useful work. (A French obstetrician once remarked that flow-charting was the most effective delivery-room analgesic he had ever seen.) One reputable British software house (Freelance Programmers, Ltd.) is almost entirely made up of women, some of them working part-time from their homes. Women returning to the work force after their children are in school have been described as capable and loyal employees as well as potentially fine programmers and systems analysts. Staff turnover is no higher in installations that use female programmers and analysts, though salary levels tend to be a trifle lower, equal-pay laws notwithstanding. Furthermore (for those who mistrust programmers' hirsute fancies), bearded female programmers are virtually unknown, despite the democratic propensities of the profession.

The strong case for inside recruiting can be illustrated with a classic case history.[2] In 1957 Britain's National Coal Board was about to embark on its first major computerization activities. Very early in the planning, it brought the Clerical and Administrative Workers' Union into the discussions, more as an adviser than an adversary. In the words of Tudor Thomas, assistant general secretary of the union: "The staff were going to be affected in at least four ways—selection, training and retraining, redeployment of displaced staff, and compensation for people who had not been absorbed into the new complex."

Instead of concentrating on the compensation issue, the union participated heartily in all four aspects. The first step was to tell people well in advance that computers were coming in. "Too often computer activity starts on the basis of rumor," says Thomas. "It is better to tell the staff at the beginning what will be computerized and when. Otherwise you get a very emotive atmosphere. We spend too much time tracking down prejudices and telling employees the plans their company management should have communicated to them long before."

An agreement for selection procedures, particularly for systems analysts, was one of the earliest joint steps. Then the Coal Board and the union made arrangements for redeploying staff, including detailed surveillance of recruiting and transfers. Employees were given two categories of notice: up to three months (depending on length of service) indication that a specific job would disappear when the computer came in; and another three months after the computer arrived for phasing out the job. This not only provided people for backup and adequate notice for the staff, but it also funneled greater management and union effort into in-company redeployment. These periods were also used to retrain staff. A system of paid time off for outside job interviews was introduced for those who could not be absorbed, and payments for these people were also negotiated. (In 1959, when the Coal Board's computer came in, there were no legal requirements for redundancy pay.) Out of 450 people affected by the computerization, only two women took the redundancy pay. They didn't wish to travel to a new location 20 miles away.

"The introduction of EDP took place in a better atmosphere and

2. The National Coal Board recruiting plan was described by Tudor Thomas at a 1971 conference in London, sponsored by Business Intelligence Services, 80 Blackfriars Road, London SE1. Proceedings are available from BIS.

staff morale was better because of these policies," says Thomas. "People had a sense of adventure. They were keen to make the system work. The chance to become senior people in the new system was important. We have applied the same criteria in subsequent conversions to newer generations of computers. The Coal Board now has twelve third-generation computers, a very efficient service, and a widely used commercial bureau."

HOW TO HIRE THEM

More than half the companies surveyed by the British Institute of Management[3] had five or less systems analysts, five or less operators, 10 or less programmers, and 25 or less data preparation people. This size department can create a constant staffing strain, but it can seldom justify a personnel specialist of its own. The DP manager and his superiors will inevitably be involved in personnel selection.

The magnificent auto mechanic need not have an automotive engineering degree. His ability to diagnose the carburetor trouble from the sound of the engine is based on experience, not theory.

Many companies are beginning to specify degrees in computer science for systems analyst candidates—perhaps because a few educational institutions are beginning to turn out computer science graduates. A handful are beginning to offer a combination of computer science and business, but results of these curricula are not yet evident. Whatever the educational trend, insisting that computer people must be graduates at all is probably a mistake, one that will severely limit the choice of good people. There is certainly room in the computer business for the graduate, but there is also a place for the individual without such credentials whose work experience is pertinent to the company or the computer.

There are several competent tests for programming aptitude—still something of a black art to discover. Several show high correlation to perception of spatial relations; they all correlate to intelligence. IBM has a test that has stood up fairly well over the years. A different but well-proved one is available from the Brandon organization.[4]

3. This is the same British Institute of Management survey that was discussed in Chapter 1.
4. The Brandon examinations are available from BIS, 80 Blackfriars Road, London SE 1, or from Brandon Applied Systems, 1700 Broadway, New York 10019.

Watch out for applicants with spurious credentials from the expensive private programming schools. They may be extremely distressed to find that their certificates are not instantly acceptable. Because there are sufficient numbers of questionable schools, it is probably wise to screen all applicants by means of a reputable aptitude test. Don't make high scores on the test the primary criterion though. It should be a screening aid rather than a selection tool. Attitudes, experience, and references are much more to the point.

Staff members get terribly frustrated when they see their company advertising for computer people "under 25." Older people inside and outside the company are perfectly able to assimilate new knowledge. Age levels may figure in the final selection, but it would be unwise to have them appear in advertisements. This discourages capable people from applying, from within or without.

If computer openings are advertised inside, you may get excellent results without further effort, with applicants whose employment records are known. The computer can open up promotion paths for more than computer people; computerization also creates direct job opportunities in other departments, and when people move to the computer department from inside, their former positions can be filled from within. In addition, many employees will begin to regard computer experience as a desirable part of more general career development.

A final comment: the computer can help you get the best out of *all* your people. The use of existing personnel says something to other employees of the company. Many contracts and benefits depend on the employee's length of service. Pension rights are seldom fully transferable. The time and money spent in recruiting from existing employees is a good investment in public relations and enhanced loyalty to the company on the part of all its employees, not just the few who move into the computer department.

Computer experience is pleasant, but seldom essential when you are staffing up a new department from the bottom. For sudden replacements, it may be necessary to go outside, but voluntary in-plant training can enhance computer usage while it identifies promising successors. First-generation computer people, incidentally, are seldom the best choice to run third-generation computers, so take claims of 20 years pertinent experience with the proverbial grain of salt.

HOW TO KEEP THEM

Computer people are constitutionally overpaid. These inflated DP salaries cause an imbalance with respect to the rest of the company; they make it harder for people at all levels to flow back and forth from user departments to the computer department. This isolation also adds to the romantic nonsense with which noncomputer people regard the mysterious machine.

For trained people from outside with pertinent experience, you will certainly have to pay a premium. Even if you hire from inside and train your own people, they will have to rise toward the national norm if you are to have any hope of retaining them. A leveling of the demand-supply pressure and the increased use of in-plant training will eventually ease this strain—which is little consolation if your chief systems analyst has just been lured away and the only candidates are looking somewhat disdainful about the size of your offers.

Profit-sharing schemes have seldom been extended to computer people, yet they may be one way of creating loyalty and identification among this self-motivated group. Opportunities for continued education may pay off in reducing personnel turnover as well as improving the computer's performance. If a small computer group feels it has profit-and-loss responsibility and authority for its own achievements, it is more likely to be cohesive and hang onto its own members than a larger group of dispersed individuals, dumbly doing the bidding of others in an authoritarian atmosphere.

When you have computer people, you frequently find that their fidelity is to the computer industry, rather than to the employer. Computer people are not so motivated by money as their high pay scales might imply. New puzzles to solve, intellectual challenge, and congenial surroundings are often more important. Philip Dorn suggests that centralization can often help: "In bigger centers your percentage of really competent people may be no higher, but you have a better chance of getting two or three good ones together. You need this kind of nucleus to develop more. When you only have one really good computer man, he is likely to drift off. In a larger center you will also get a large number of mediocre people—the computing field is full of mediocre people."

In a small or dispersed organization, the single star will most often drift off to a bureau or software house, which offers more diversity and challenge. The centralized computer department, operating in competition with outside bureaus and software companies for the business of its not-quite-captive users, can often retain such people by virtue of the more interesting work, as well as the intellectual stimulus of working with other good computer people.

It may be no coincidence that one company with an error/rerun rate consistently under 4 percent and sometimes under 2 percent also has a low staff turnover and exceptionally high involvement from user departments. These assign one or two people full-time to the computer department for the duration of a project. This flow of users into the computer department is healthy. Even healthier, but harder to bring about because of the disparity in salaries, is a flow of competent computer people into the company management. Though this would offer new career prospects to people who otherwise feel they have reached a plateau, the cost to retain them by moving them into other departments is awfully high if it means all management pay scales have to shift upward. One solution may be to demand six months doing noncomputer work in a user department as part of the systems analyst training.

If you accept the premise that the systems analyst should first of all be oriented toward the business rather than the computer, then systems analysis could also come to be regarded as an in-company training ground for middle managers. This would not only build more corporate loyalty in a constitutionally disenfranchised group, but would also attract candidates rather painlessly for the computer department.

Computers are becoming more important in corporate plans. As a result, more top managers are beginning to talk directly to their computer specialists. Too often these communications fail abysmally because the transmitter and the receiver are tuned to dreadfully different vocabularies. Nonetheless, more day-to-day work is being done on computers, and more management decisions are based on information that comes from the computer people. Communications are improving, and will get still better as the flow between departments increases.

The McKinsey report relates the involvement of line managers in user departments with the success of a computer installation. McKinsey's definition of success takes into account the return on a computer investment that can be measured (though frequently the greatest benefits are intangible), the range of useful applications, and the satisfaction of the chief executive. Figure 13-1 shows a startlingly close relationship between this line-management involvement at every stage of application development and the overall success of the installation.

The corollary to management involvement with computers is logically computer department involvement with management.

The systems analyst may be the key to resolving some of the communications problems as well as organizational problems. A young systems analyst has not quite priced himself out of the middle-management market—yet. Computer departments are getting more centralized, but there is also a need for dispersed experts, more or less resident in major user departments. If the computer department is mature enough to work on a "matrix" basis, with dispersed analysts, responsible ultimately to the computer manager or chief systems analyst, but operationally part of their user departments, everybody can benefit. The users have full-time representation. The computer department has a trusted member translating its needs. The systems analysts may vanish; they have a chance to assimilate noncomputer problems and choose career paths in general management. Others can be created to take their place. The company ultimately spends less and may get more for its computer investment.

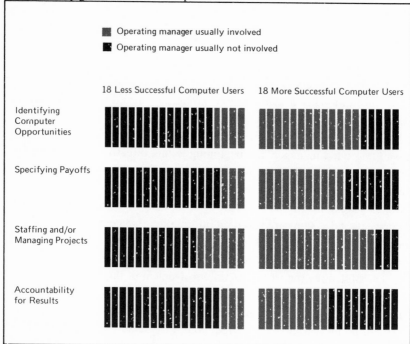

Fig. 13-1. Management involvement versus computer success. Source: McKinsey & Co.

14

Training for High Payoff

How do most people learn to drive? Some take courses. Others learn from a friend or relative. Whatever the source, there are certain factors that make a difference in the eventual driving skill:

- the patience and communicating skill of the instructor
- the confidence and attention of the student
- a healthy balance between the theory and rules and practical experience on the road
- the absence of stone walls and blind corners
- the chance to practice what has been preached

Drivers get rusty without practice, or they fall into lazy habits that can be dangerous. To make sure that everybody on the road has reached a minimum standard for safety, the British government licenses drivers. It sets higher standards for truck drivers or chauffeurs. Learners have limitations to protect themselves and their passengers as well as other people on the road. No one has yet suggested a passenger license, but bouncing children, clinging girls, and bossy mothers-in-law have often received ad hoc training.

There are passengers, private drivers, and chauffeurs in computing, too. All of them benefit from proper training.

Computer training and computer education are different things. Most purists prefer to use the term *computer education* (or *computer-assisted education*) to refer to the use of computers in schools, often as an adjunct to other subjects. Since a business is not a schoolroom, we will use the term *computer training* to discuss the entire spectrum of training courses, seminars, conferences, or teaching aids that are available to help companies get more out of their computers or the people using them.

THE FEAR FACTOR

It should be clear by now that the computer, quite an elegant creature on occasion, has suffered from bad press, too much jargon from its keepers, and too little comfortable contact with its owners. By the end of the sixties, it was evident that management involvement was much more important to the successful installation than any nuances of computer technology. But involving managers means talking to them and *listening* to them—something too few internal computer departments were able to do. The classic case of paying lip service to management involvement by fielding a three-day computer appreciation course too often resolves itself with the managers nodding sagely, saying "Involvement is A Good Thing," but firmly resisting any attempts to change things in their own departments.

The cause may be neither fear nor distrust—simply inertia, a common characteristic among humans. We all tend to resist change. But inertia at the user department level can be overcome—it just takes a lot of energy, and sometimes mass as well. The manager needs to see that *his* management is involved in the project. He needs further training in the specific kinds of changes that are coming in. He needs long, comfortable discussions with his own computer man (who in turn should be trained to speak business English to him). No project can really get under way until the primary line manager has accepted the need for it.

The fear factor sets up not just passive resistance but sometimes irrational stone walls of opposition, at many levels. Too many people have heard Orwellian stories about jobs being eliminated by computers. The specter of the automated factory still haunts union leaders. The truth is somewhat different. Jobs may be automated, but others are created just as fast. A computer salesman of some repute once commented that he had never sold a machine that put anybody out of work. When Britain's National Coal Board computerized in the late fifties, only two out of the 450 affected employees were laid off, and even those two had been offered alternate and interesting jobs.

Training is the key to this shifting balance of jobs. It is also the first line of defense against the fear factor, which always stems from rumor, half-truths, and unknown bogeymen. When people know from their own management what the computer plans are and exactly how their jobs and organizations will be affected, much of the fear evaporates. When a new computer is contemplated, recruiting from within helps allay fears. When a new application is going to affect a department, early familiarization and training can make the implementation job much easier. Computer appreciation courses, not only for top management but also for middle management and shop-floor people, can make it clear that the computer is not capable of original thought. When the machine can be viewed as a piece of machinery, designed, built, and run by human beings, it won't seem as threatening or big-brotherish.

There is a generation gap as well as a jargon barrier. Younger employees are much more likely to view the incoming machine as an opportunity. Older ones may consciously or subconsciously fear it more, seeing their retirement hastened or their advancement jeopardized by the incomprehensible monster. The computer's intrusion on human mysteries is important too. Many employees mask their feelings of inadequacy by mumbo jumbo, making secret and mystical the procedures for their fairly straightforward jobs. The threat that an all-seeing computer could reveal all may be particularly terrifying. The opportunity to master new secrets may help avoid major resistance from such people—who may be quite capable despite their anxieties.

If you are expecting to find fears among your people when computers are introduced, you may be better armored with training tools to cope with them. The fears will continue to occur, in smaller concentrations, whenever the computer is used in a new way. The computer appreciation course (the more specific the better) is your first line of defense.

APPRECIATING COMPUTERS

Computer appreciation courses are usually designed for busy top managers, who zip through "What-is-a-computer?" and a potted rundown of languages, coming out the other end with a few new buzzwords and sometimes an easier attitude about the machine. If the course has been conducted in-house, the managers may also emerge with some respect for their own computer people (a major achievement).

The choice of instructors for such courses is critical. They must be able to talk to managers in their own language. The courses themselves should be kept fairly informal, with room for discussion, disagreement, and interaction. This, too, demands a special kind of instructor.

In the computer profitability survey published by the British Institute of Management, most companies recognized the need for preparing the ground, but 11 percent of the 102 companies responding had no appreciation courses at all. About a third of the companies had courses run by computer manufacturers; another third were run by the computer company teamed with inside people; 16 percent had courses planned and run internally; and the remaining 8 percent were presented by consultants. Most companies (76 percent) felt that their courses had been fairly successful; 8 percent felt that they had been unsuccessful; 16 percent were completely satisfied with the results. The consultant courses were regarded as wholly successful by two out of the five who had them—a record twice as good as the others, but based on a very small sample.

Courses from the computer manufacturers are usually quite competent, as these opinions indicate, but they suffer from one pervasive problem: they overstress the hardware and gadgetry, at the expense of the basic principles, the human elements, and the ways computers are used in business. They also tend to take the view that the computers solve problems; a more realistic coverage of some of the problems they *create* might be more helpful.

About 80 percent of the companies surveyed had courses for senior and middle management; 50 percent had courses for supervisors; only 25 percent ran courses for other levels of staff.

Appreciation courses for lower-level management and clerical or shop-floor people are less common, but they are undoubtedly a sound investment, particularly if you have invested in your own tailored curriculum for top management. This can often be amended to be taught by the same instructor, with less management implications and more shop-floor procedure. The same communication and interaction skills are necessary in the instructor, though the dialect may be different. It is safe (indeed, necessary) to assume that the staff are not materially less intelligent than top management, particularly when it gets down to details of the system in the shop. If the key systems analyst also sits in on this type of course to answer specific questions, he can sometimes benefit from practical suggestions from the people who actually understand in detail the tasks to be computerized.

It is seldom possible to send an entire department or group on a computer appreciation course; such functions as production or invoicing might cease entirely. Scheduling extended lunch-hour seminars for small groups works fairly well. Instead of stressing management involvement, personnel problems, and project control, the course can concentrate on the specific applications, opportunities for new jobs, and what the system will do for the department and the company. Definitions of the main buzzwords and descriptions of retraining plans will allay many fears.

ENTRY-LEVEL TRAINING

When a company decides to train its own programmers or operators from inside, it is undertaking a major project. Several computer manufacturers can provide curriculum assistance and training aids. One (Control Data Corporation) has for many years maintained an entry-level training company (Control Data Institute) that provides adequate screening, full-time training, and relatively successful placement of graduates. Technical colleges are also improving their curricula for entry-level computer jobs.

There are a number of commercial schools for keypunch operators, computer operators, or commercial programmers that do *not* meet these criteria. Screening is often negligible—tantamount to a credit check. Students are enticed to invest large sums by promises of highly paid jobs, but are seldom properly trained for good positions. One young woman applied for a keypunch job armed with a graduation certificate from one such school stating that she was proficient on seven different types of equipment. She had never seen six of them, and did not realize what her certificate promised. (She was fortunately absorbed into in-plant training by the outraged personnel man.)

Setting up an in-house program requires at the very least a professional training officer; he may be backed up with consultants, temporary or volunteer instructors, or the loan of specialists from different departments. It is sometimes possible to farm out the entire job to a consultancy. Since IBM unbundled, computer training has grown into a thriving little subindustry; a number of firms offer canned or tailored courses that are quite competent. It may be sufficient simply to screen applicants for entry-level operator or programmer jobs quite carefully, then send them outside to a competent organization for further screening and training. The initial cost is high, but this can cut the internal overhead and allow the in-house training budget to be concentrated on other elements of the company.

THE MAKE-OR-BUY DECISION

There is a strong case to be made for in-house training. This revolves around one fundamental point: the training can be tailored. Not only are courses tailored to the problems and applications that are crucial to the company, but they are also tailored to the particular interests of the people being trained. Examples or case studies are more pertinent. Company management is inevitably more involved. Furthermore, the use of an outside consultant/instructor to help develop the course can bring about improvements in internal procedures. One of the most important benefits comes in improved internal communications.

The case against in-house training revolves around the allocation of human and fiscal resources. Tailor-made courses cost more initially; self-generated instructors are taken away from their primary jobs; someone must schedule the facilities and times, in conflict with other company demands. Unless in-house training is well coordinated and carefully overseen, it can be messy and more nuisance than help to all concerned. Nonetheless, for the relatively orderly company that can cope with these things, I favor this approach over all others.

People learn only when they begin using what they've studied. With an in-house course, people can get answers immediately as they try to apply the techniques they are being taught. When employees come back from outside courses, they often realize that some fundamental point was missed, or not covered. But by that time the teacher is no longer accessible. The in-house instructor can bridge this chasm between theory and practice.

In-house training is logical for another reason. You don't waste time talking about things that don't apply to your own company. Furthermore, a public course has a strong tendency to be self-centered, with the trainer saying what he wants to say rather than what the trainee wants to hear.

These general observations have different aspects in the training of operators, programmers, systems analysts, and general management.

OPERATOR TRAINING

The transition from a training environment to the real world should be evolutionary, not a leap into the unknown. This is how experts have trained people from taxi drivers to keypunch operators to chairmen for decades. First they analyze the skills that are needed for the job. Then they develop these skills in the trainees. Finally they build stamina. This means the ability to do the job as a whole, not just separate parts of it, and the ability to keep on doing it. The classic example is the keypunch operator who can go a hundred miles an hour for the first part of the day, then disintegrates after her coffee break.

The production side has been the Cinderella of computing. Systems and programming often seem like the well-to-do older sisters who have grabbed most of the limelight. But some astonishing things can happen in operations efficiency when this kind of training is done in-house.

Typically, computer operators don't get proper training to begin with. Thus it is not surprising that they develop haphazard ways. This situation seems to be getting worse for the operators as life gets simpler for the programmers. The fancier operating systems on new computers, for example, make it harder for the operators themselves to keep track of what is going on. So do disk systems, though they don't usually require the operators to run around as much as they had to in tape installations. The latest computer consoles look like the controls for a 747; the average operator gets mildly hysterical when he sees all those buttons and lights; he also worries when they turn red.

Operations management is another problem area that can be helped with in-plant training. A complex computer calls for a good manager, not a has-been programmer. He needs training to understand the human aspects of his job as well as the nuances of the computer. There may be shift work; it is often quite dull and repetitive working in a computer room; production control and scheduling are ongoing problems. The operations manager may make decisions 40 or 50 times a day that affect the profitability of the installation. Programmers and systems people make these kinds of decisions two or three times a week.

The training man who comes into the operations room, whether he is an internal specialist in a large company or an outside consultant, can also offer an auditor's view of the existing procedures. As a trainer, he can bring about major changes. It is a simple but persistent situation. The work is repetitive, so bad habits get established easily and ingrained deeply. It is also an environment that tends to have one-time input and multiple outputs, so the effects of these sloppy habits are multiplied.

Though operators often receive training, people responsible for input to the computer—the clerks, administrators, secretaries, and supervisors in user departments—seldom get much attention. Short seminars in computer operation, preferably with people from the computer room in attendance, can pay off handsomely.

Operations training suffers particularly if it takes place in a vacuum—before the computer has been installed. Although advance notice and growing familiarization are necessary, as in any training, a time-lag that is too great between the training and the practice erases some of the value of the training. Regular refresher courses for operators and their managers can pay for themselves quickly.

PROGRAMMER TRAINING

Training must relate to the job the man is going to do. It should cover the "why" before it goes into the "how." This means a programmer training course should look at the reasons for having computers before it considers flow-charting. And flow-charting should be understood before students get to coding. If they look at the program as a whole before they worry about how many instructions can be saved in a certain subroutine, they may be less likely to underoptimize—a common programmer practice by which optimizing in one part (having an assembly-language routine, for example, in a high-level language program) makes it impossible to optimize the whole program properly. This is also true between programs, when one giant program may be very well optimized within itself, but brings an entire multiprogramming installation to a halt while it hogs all the resources.

Learning to code, test, and document real programs is more important initially than finding out what each instruction does. Testing and documentation are often learned rather offhandedly from colleagues who may have very bad habits indeed. The trainee who does not encounter the proper procedures in a course has no choice but to copy his neighbor's methods. By starting properly, he may even help sharpen up the habits of his new neighbors when he gets down to work.

Once again, with an in-house program, the transition from training to work can be gradual. Course assignments deal with company projects and are carried out according to the company's own programming standards, rather than to an externally imposed, too-general set. The languages taught are exactly the ones the fledgling programmers will be using. With their own languages, their own standards, their own computer configuration, and their own applications under scrutiny throughout the training phase, they can usually make the transition to everyday work fairly gracefully.

SYSTEMS ANALYST TRAINING

As with programmers, most companies who have given the matter any thought prefer to have their systems analysts trained to the company's own standards, dealing with its own projects, in addition to meeting professional standards for systems analysis. They want not just guidelines but specifics.

In-house training for systems analysts is also more concentrated. There tend to be fewer analysts in any one installation, so classes are usually smaller. Therefore, they get *tuition,* not just lectures. One pertinent case study can be worth 1000 hours of generalized lectures. The Bloggs course can evolve around production scheduling for Bloggs Widgets, not linear programming for a North Sea oil exploration company. A firm with problems in warehousing and distribution was able to have a course structured to its own needs, with special attention to software packages for transportation and vehicle scheduling, then some pertinent operations research techniques, but without an unnecessary full-scale OR course.

Repeatability is another important aspect of in-house training for analysts. If a reputable consultant is designing the course for you and presenting the first session, he can also train some of your senior people to repeat the course later, when you need new analysts. This may be a very simple matter (at negligible cost) of having the potential in-house trainers sit in on the first session and study the curriculum. (The transition is sometimes easier if you have the original consultant back to keep an eye on the first internally presented course and assist the new instructors as necessary.) Training for your own instructors (or systems analysts in general) can take much more elaborate forms. Residential "communications" courses are available in which small groups gather for role playing and an investigation of good and bad techniques for communicating, interviewing, teaching, or selling. Although these sessions can be very expensive, less intensive versions can be arranged for in-house presentation.

Internal training courses for systems analysts can also be comfortable and useful places for cross-fertilization. If a member of the Management Services or OR group attends the course, he will not only learn more about the computer, but inevitably teach the potential analysts about the services available to them from this group. A user department with a major application under way can send a student who brings his own case study. The personnel man may have more insight into the mysteries of systems analysis if he attends a course. He may also bring valuable insights into the human aspects of this important job.

MANAGEMENT TRAINING AND DEVELOPMENT

General managers are invariably busy, under pressure, easily distracted by day-to-day problems. Often they complain that outside courses are only half-relevant to their own jobs. In-house training for management carries a different danger: constant interruptions will distract them unless they are as firmly buffered from the everyday problems as if they were away at a course. Once this problem can be solved, many prefer the in-company training courses geared toward their own industry and company problems and structure.

To do in-house training effectively, you need an optimum number of people in each course. If the chairman is going to pick the instructor's brains all alone, he might as well call him a consultant and pay less for the privilege. Thus, for some specifics like DP management, it is sometimes cheaper to send the one or two DP managers out to a course where they can exchange views with their counterparts in other companies.

In addition to appreciation courses, management development courses with computer content are well suited to in-house presentation. These can evaluate management style or train junior and middle managers in new techniques, especially if these are being implemented company-wide. Junior managers in particular are often overlooked when training for a future computer is planned. These in-house meetings, without going all the way to T-Groups and Encounters, usually improve internal communications as managers find their counterparts in other departments coping with similar problems. It is sometimes possible in the course of such meetings (if they cover a wide spectrum of management) for the company itself to adapt to newly revealed needs of its managers. This is seldom possible when such courses are attended outside.

Nothing is more disheartening than to return from an exhilarating outside seminar on decision tables or some other interesting new technique and meet a solid wall of resistance back in the company. This kind of corporate lip service to management science just wastes money and manpower. It can also cause good men to go elsewhere. A much higher payoff comes from internal seminars, with sufficient weight to bring about changes, to consider the new techniques—operations research, linear programming, DCF evaluations, modeling, forecasting, statistics, decision tables, games theory. All these can be useful, and would merit discussion around a table of mixed technologists and managers.

They can be overdone. "Games theory doesn't help you play games, and decision theory doesn't help you make up your mind," says Dr. Maurice Kendall, himself a first-class statistician. "The courses which purport to teach scientific management often teach science, but not management."

THE COST OF TRAINING

Most computer users spend about 2 percent of their annual computing budgets on computer-related training—or so they think. This sum doesn't include the frequent waste of management time, not only in the computer department but throughout the company, that can be attributed to sorting out problems or misunderstandings in which the computer department (with its separate vocabulary) played some part. Nor does it include the unquantifiable cost of poor standards, operations procedures, or programmers—which can be a frightening sum if you recall that a bad programmer can take 25 times as long to write his program, then slop up five times as much storage and 15 times as much computer time as a good programmer doing the same job. Granted that good programmers can be viewed as Gifts of God, training can still make the difference between very bad and quite adequate programmers.

So the cost of not-training should be added to the cost of training, if anyone can quantify it. In this context, the investment in a capable training officer may look more attractive. It is seldom necessary to have an entire training department, but a single knowledgeable coordinator, reporting high enough to focus corporate activities, can pay for himself. A well-coordinated in-house training program, for example, can weed out the professional course-goer in the systems analysis group and get him back to doing real work. Centralized planning can coordinate courses or seminars with proposed applications. Training aids developed for a course in one department can be used for others. It may be possible to improve the flow of slides and charts back and forth between marketing, advertising, documentation and training groups.

The central training officer may save money as a source of information about external courses and the availability of government grants for training. In many companies the grants are negotiated from a central financial point, while DP departments and others have separate budgets for training. They often choose cheaper courses that don't qualify for grants, rather than seemingly more expensive ones that actually cost less (and often give more) after the grant has been deducted from the cost.

If the training officer is given his own budget, he should not be expected to show a large profit. The benefits of a training program are diffuse, hard to quantify, but extend over many years. Excessive charges on an internal accounting basis could hamper the effectiveness of a program.

Much of the manpower required to teach a diversity of courses is already available within the company and can be developed by a persuasive training officer. An unpolished performer who knows his subject well and can communicate it in simple terms is a better investment than the most polished professor who is trying to teach a subject he doesn't really understand. Incidentally, ex-IBM people usually make excellent instructors. They receive exceptionally fine training in communications skills at IBM; members of this species can usually be recognized by their fondness for flip-charts and fluency on their feet.

Employees often blossom when they are asked to conduct a course. They regard this as a mark of management recognition, and work hard to polish their material. It is wise to give in-house people considerable advance notice, to check up regularly on their progress, and to offer assistance with visual aids. The reassuring presence of a training officer who can take over in extremis will help guard against stage fright in maiden appearances. (Small groups and interaction are also helpful here.) There will inevitably be poor communicators if courses are developed from inside, but the overall benefits can justify the risk.

When a comprehensive training program has been established, there will eventually be students who wish to continue their studies toward a degree. A number of companies have made part-time-plus-scholarship arrangements, or even full-time leave with pay, to encourage these employees. IBM, for example, maintains a Systems Research Institute in New York that offers a full-time 13-week resident course for senior systems people. Arrangements were eventually made with the prestigious Polytechnic Institute of Brooklyn to give graduates of the IBM computer science course a full six credits toward a Master of Science degree. Students must apply for graduate standing and take a PIB examination at the end of the course in order to qualify.

This kind of academic/industrial cooperation is increasing. If your training program is already established and working well, it might be worth discussing cooperative needs and interests with a nearby college or university.

No company can live in a vacuum, and no training program can depend entirely on in-house ventures. Contact with outside colleagues is important, not only for the DP manager, but for many other managers and specialists. Though the benefit of large computer conferences or industry gatherings sometimes seems more social than actual, these meetings keep new ideas flowing into a company. Some people thrive on the exhilarating exposure. Others wilt under the stress. It should be possible to achieve a balance, so that most middle managers and systems analysts who want to will be able to attend certain outside events (as departmental budgets permit) on a fair rotation basis. Gaggles of salesmen and glorious exhibits seldom justify their cost. (IBM itself has eliminated exhibits and cut down attendance at the major Joint Computer Conferences in the United States, though there are still numerous IBM men carefully taking notes as they wander around other people's exhibits.)

If it is impossible to buffer managers from interruptions on in-house courses, residential courses may be justified. Costs and results are not always clearly related. Some charge exorbitant fees for "name" speakers, who attract large audiences, thereby cutting down the chances for discussion. Bring in the expert, instead, and pick his brains for a day or two. The cost may be less than sending two men away. A small, special-purpose residential course can be a good investment. One company reports that it can handle transportation and comfortable accommodations to such exotic places as Tenerife for the same cost as local courses. The training company piously maintains that the courses are sufficiently stressful so that students benefit from having proper recreational facilities, not just alcoholic refreshment during breaks. Whether a swim or a scotch does more to restore the weary student may be debatable, but these courses also attract first-class guest instructors, and interruptions from anxious secretaries are negligible in Bermuda (or Long Island, for that matter).

SOURCES FOR COURSES

"Canned" course materials are coming into common use, and can provide useful starter-kits for in-house courses or backup for companies that use a broad spectrum of courses.

The most convenient canned courses seem to be those that are produced on videotape. Some are available from specialist companies. The investment is quite small—a few hundred dollars a month at most—for a videotape player and a TV set plus study guides and about 16 reels of half-hour courses. Most of these videotape courses are based on an IBM curriculum and the IBM documentation that is already available to 360 installations. Computer manufacturers themselves (notably Honeywell) are beginning to develop videotape courses of their own. Students can use this kind of course as time is available, with quizzes (scored by a course coordinator) to check progress. Any point that is not clear at first can be reviewed with the tape and the documentation until it is understood. There is no live instructor or class full of colleagues from whom to hide one's ignorance.

Magnetic tape and movie film or slide-projector visual aids are also available with packaged computer courses. All of these depend on the quality of the instructor. The most impressive teachers seem to me to be working programmers.

As the primary training medium, packaged courses alone leave something to be desired: discussion. For special techniques and technical subjects, or even for computer appreciation, they can be fairly adequate, but they seem to work much better when they are reinforced with live discussions and pertinent case studies.

All the computer makers offer competent courses dealing with their own computers and languages. Applications-specific courses are also available in some areas. IBM sometimes convenes groups of users (and potential users) in specific industries or with specific applications such as production control for two-day or three-day courses. These are rewarding for their specific content and the high population of users experienced in the subject. They are also serious and useful gatherings; any invitation to attend one should not be regarded as a boondoggle.

Courses from the computer manufacturers are less likely to deal with the human or technical problems of computing than are the consultant or training company courses. They are also less likely to be suited to in-house presentation, though some cooperative ventures can be classed as successful. A consultant company that has a management bias instead of a hardware bias may be better suited to helping set up a training program or a specific course. The number of choices will grow as more companies enter the training field, and more users realize that training has a high payoff in computer profitability.

Index